THE HAN
FICTION WORKBOOK

An Activity-Based Approach
to Fiction Writing

EDWARD ALLEN
San Jose State University

Prentice Hall, Upper Saddle River, NJ 07458

Editorial/production supervision: Editorial Services of New England/Rojean Wagner
Acquisitions editor: Alison Reeves
Interior design: Editorial Services of New England
Cover design: Bruce Kenselaar
Manufacturing buyer: Lynn Pearlman

© 1996 by Prentice-Hall, Inc.
Simon & Schuster/A Viacom Company
Upper Saddle River, NJ 07458

Printed in the United States of America
10   9   8   7   6   5   4   3   2   1

ISBN 0-13-238882-0

Prentice-Hall International (UK) Limited, London
Prentice-Hall of Australia Pty. Limited, Sydney
Prentice-Hall Canada Inc., Toronto
Prentice-Hall Hispanoamericana, S.A., Mexico
Prentice-Hall of India Private Limited, New Delhi
Prentice-Hall of Japan, Inc., Tokyo
Simon & Schuster Asia Pte. Ltd., Singapore
Editora Prentice-Hall do Brasil, Ltda., Rio de Janeiro

To my Father

Are you lost daddy I arsked tenderly.
Shut up he explained.

—Ring Lardner, "The Young Immigrunts"

Contents

Acknowledgments

I want to thank the following teachers, colleagues, and friends whose help contributed, directly or indirectly, to this workbook: Paul Nelson, Barry Goldensohn, Jack Matthews, Jack Pulaski, Pam Durban, Wayne Dodd, Juris Jurjevics, Irene Skolnick, Gerry Howard, Pat Strachan, Dan Menaker, Thomas Mallon, Amy Wilson, Kit Givan, Piotr Pienkowski, Barbara and Brendon Bernard. Special thanks to Anne Allen and William Bernard for the illustration on page 68.

Introduction

You don't have to read this introduction if you don't want to. In fact, if you're the kind of person who likes to skip introductions, that's a healthy sign. It's good to want to get started and to get right into the activity section of the book. So I won't hold you up too long.

If you've ever heard a joke and wanted to improve on it, if you've ever enjoyed scaring your friends with a ghost story, if you've ever gotten a thrill out of fooling someone with a lie then you have participated in one of the most ancient of human traditions, the tradition of storytelling. Everything from bedtime stories to *Moby-Dick* is part of this tradition.

This is a workbook, meaning that you won't get much out of it if you just read it and put it aside. You need to do the exercises in the chapters, and you need to keep your scrapbook current.

If you're using this book in a class, you have a ready-made schedule to follow. If you're using the book on your own, you'll have to improvise. What I've found is that most people need some sort of definite schedule. In the first chapter I'll talk about finding a schedule that works for you.

You'll also have to do some outside reading. You've probably noticed that this skinny book doesn't contain any short stories for class discussion. Rather than just read stories from the textbook, you'll be expected to put together your own reading program, which I'll talk about in Chapter 2.

If you're nervous about submitting work to be judged by strangers, I don't know what to tell you, except that it gets easier as you go along. And a good class, an honest class, becomes a kind of support group, in which the worst thing that can happen to you is that somebody will say, "Y'know, this is really pretty bad."

We've all had that experience. I won't deny that it hurts. But you get over it. And then when something you write does work, and people in class like it, you'll know they're telling the truth.

For those readers not using the book as part of a class, I urge you to find some other kind of support system, consisting of friends and colleagues who can give you some feedback. It's possible to work in a vacuum, but it's always easier with friends. And remember that as an independent amateur you're the prime target for all kinds of scams aimed at fledgling writers. Guard your checkbook.

Well, maybe you're not reading this anyway. That's okay. But I just want to say in all seriousness that everything I could think of to help your writing is in here. I hope it works for you. Good luck.

Edward Allen

1

❖

What You Need to Get Started

PURPOSE OF CHAPTER

The purpose of this chapter is to help you assemble the things you need to get started writing. Some of these things are physical possessions; but just as important at this time are the mental habits you establish and the decisions you make.

Just so you and your instructor are sure about what resources you will be working with, the next few pages are set up as a questionnaire. Your instructor will look over your answers, and if any of them seem unrealistic, you can talk about it. If you are working independently, you should still do this questionnaire, as well as all the others in this book.

THE BASIC TOOLS

Compared to skiing, private aviation, or rock and roll, writing is not a particularly capital-intensive pursuit. True, a word processor is considered the tool of choice, but that technology gets cheaper every day. And plenty of successful writers get by perfectly well on typewriters.

If you haven't used word processing before and plan to start, this is a good time to ask your instructor and classmates what they would recommend. Remember that the software (the word processing program) is just as important as the hardware (the computer and its related equipment). Most writers love to talk about their systems, so you can expect to get some helpful information from them . . . perhaps more than you really want.

In addition to a writing tool, you will need a place where you can work undisturbed, and a block of uninterrupted time, preferably every day. For many people, especially people with children, these are the hardest things of all to come by. Do your best, and use your imagination. Some people work better in the morning; some favor the afternoon or the wee hours. Remember that it doesn't have to be a huge block of time. Even ten minutes a day, every day, is better than two hours once a week. Momentum is everything.

Use your imagination. What can you reschedule? What can you give up? What priorities can you reorder? Remember that a writer has to be a little bit selfish. Now is the time to start developing that selfishness.

A QUESTIONNAIRE ABOUT GETTING STARTED

Tools

1. What are you writing with? (Describe software, hardware, and printer.)

   _____

   _____

2. How proficient are you in using your software? If you are using a typewriter, how good a typist are you?

   _____

   _____

   _____

Working Space

3. Do you have a private place to write on a daily basis? Where is it?

   _____

   _____

Time

4. What time of the day do you think you are at your best?

   _____

5. How much time daily do you think you can give to your writing?

   _____

   _____

6. What problems or obligations present the greatest obstacle to your daily writing schedule?

   _____

   _____

7. What can you do to overcome those obstacles?

   _____

   _____

   _____

SCRAPBOOK EXERCISE

In the Scrapbook Appendix at the end of this book, you'll find a place to make a list of things you want your work to do, what you want to accomplish as a writer. Fill in at least five of the spaces. You should feel free to come back to that scrapbook exercise from time to time over the semester to see if you're making progress toward accomplishing any of those goals.

SUGGESTIONS FOR CURRENT PROJECT

Now is as good a time as any to get started on your story or novel. For the time being, you need no instructions, no agenda, no plan. Just write down every thought you can think of about the project, whether or not you think you can actually use it. Right now it's more important to write than to write well. Just generate the pages—at least five pages and preferably ten. If they're terrible, and they may well be, you and your instructor and your friends will have plenty of time to ask why.

2

Your Reading Plan and Your Scrapbook

PURPOSE OF CHAPTER

This chapter is the place where you will take an inventory of your past reading and design a personal reading plan for the duration of the time when you are using this book. I will also provide a checklist of some reference books essential to all writers.

MY THEORY ABOUT WHY SO MANY CREATIVE WRITING CLASSES ARE SO BAD

Every writer needs to read, and to read with a kind of passion. Although every other rule in this book may have exceptions, if you don't read you'll never be a decent writer. Perhaps that is why so many creative writing classes are so horrible. Creative writing classes tend to attract the students who don't want to do all the reading that they would have to do in a literature course. This means, paradoxically, that the non-readers, the students with the least potential as writers, are going to flock to Creative Writing 101.

Now, if you heard yourself described in the previous paragraph, don't be discouraged. Reading is a habit that you can start at any time in your life. It's true that for people raised on television (myself included), starting any reading project tends to feel like jumping into cold water. But when you get started you'll know it's worth it. The feeling of being immersed in a book, of going through your daily routine and waiting to get home to read some more and see what happens to Emma Bovary or Hazel Motes tonight—this is a level of intimacy between life and art that even good television does not achieve.

Depending on where you are in your education (or whether you're in school at all), you might want to look into courses that cover as much literature as possible. It's not mandatory, of course, but the average novice can get much more out of taking a class in Shakespeare or Jane Austen or Toni Morrison than from puzzling through the books alone.

The crucial point here is that if you think you can be a decent writer without being a good reader, you're wasting your time. However, if you really don't want to read, I'm not going to tell you to quit writing, even though you clearly have no future. There's a good reason for that. Schools need students, and creative writing teachers need jobs; and bad writers fill the seats in a class as fully as good ones. This book needs customers to buy it, and the publisher and the author are just as willing to accept money from deadwood, nonreading writers as we are from writers with some potential.

Just let me ask you to do your instructor a favor. If you truly choose not to read, share that decision with your instructor. That way your instructor can avoid wasting time and energy on you and can concentrate on the writers who have a chance.

CHECKLIST OF BOOKS YOU NEED TO OWN

I've said before that even with the cost of computers factored in, writing is a relatively non-capital-intensive pursuit. That's true. But you will need a few reference books. Use the space provided to write down the title and edition of the books you already own.

1. First, a good dictionary, the biggest and best you can afford, and a small portable dictionary.

    _____

    _____

2. Thesaurus. Even if you have one in your computer, get the book too.

    _____

3. Fiction Anthology. You've probably noticed that this book does not include short stories for class discussion. I've always suspected that some textbooks include stories because that's the only way the students will read *anything*. You've already heard what I think about writers who don't read, so just remember that a vigorous program of outside reading is an integral part of this course.

   Unless your instructor assigns a specific anthology for the class, you should choose your own and buy it and read as much of it as you can. Get a big one, such as the *Norton Anthology of Short Fiction*, or Prentice Hall's *Literature: An Introduction to Reading and Writing*, 4th ed.

4. Writer's Handbook. Get Strunk and White's *The Elements of Style* and one other larger handbook.

Optional but Highly Recommended

1. *The Reader's Encyclopedia*, William Rose Benet, ed.
2. A current almanac.
3. The best world atlas you can find.
4. A road atlas.
5. *Bartlett's Familiar Quotations* or *The Oxford Dictionary of Quotations*.
6. The Bible (any version, but be aware that the King James Bible has probably had the most influence on literature in English). Scriptures from other religions can also be useful.
7. Reference books in your own field of interest. It doesn't matter what you care about, but you have to care about something enough to learn something about it.

A FICTON READING CHECKLIST

The books listed on the next page represent an incomplete and very opinionated sample of the novels considered part of the basic knowledge of all American writers. Remember that the list constantly changes.

Check whether you've read each book or not. Be honest; nobody but you has to see this. Besides, if you've read none of these books, that's not such a bad thing. You have more to look forward to.

Chaucer, Selections from *The Canterbury Tales*   _____

William Shakespeare, At least two plays   _____

Charles Dickens, *Great Expectations*   _____

Emily Brontë, *Wuthering Heights*   _____

Charlotte Brontë, *Jane Eyre*   _____

Herman Melville, *Moby-Dick*   _____

Kate Chopin, *The Awakening*   _____

Mark Twain, *Huckleberry Finn*   _____

Harriet Beecher Stowe, *Uncle Tom's Cabin*   _____

William Faulkner, *The Sound and the Fury*   _____

Virginia Woolf, *Mrs. Dalloway*   _____

F. Scott Fitzgerald, *The Great Gatsby*   _____

Willa Cather, *My Antonia*   _____

Sherwood Anderson, *Winesburg, Ohio*   _____

Edith Wharton, *Ethan Frome*   _____

Vladimir Nabokov, *Lolita*   _____

John Steinbeck, *The Grapes of Wrath*   _____

Flannery O'Connor, *Wise Blood*   _____

J.D. Salinger, *The Catcher in the Rye*   _____

Harper Lee, *To Kill a Mockingbird*   _____

Margaret Atwood, *The Handmaid's Tale*   _____

Louise Erdrich, *The Beet Queen*   _____

John Updike, *Rabbit, Run*   _____

Alice Walker, *The Color Purple*   _____

M. Scott Momaday, *House Made of Dawn*   _____

Toni Morrison, *Beloved*   _____

Gloria Naylor, *The Women of Brewster Place*   _____

Other Novels

List five other novels that have made an impression on you. If you can't think of five, don't worry.

1. _____
2. _____
3. _____
4. _____
5. _____

This list doesn't try to be complete. It's just a starting point for people who haven't read very much fiction. You don't have to read all the books here, but you should pick at least half of your personal reading program from the books on this list that you haven't read.

It's not that you have to read all of this (or any of this, really) to be a cultured and sensitive person. It's just that you have to read something, and unless you have a particular reading agenda pressing on you now, you might as well start with this material.

CUSTOMIZING YOUR PERSONAL READING PROGRAM

Are you using this workbook in a class? _____

If so, how long is the term of that class? _____

Include one novel *and* five short stories for every three weeks of the term. In other words, if the term is twelve weeks long, you should plan to read at least four novels and at least twenty short stories over the course of the term. You don't have to list the short stories now. Just list them as you read them.

If you are using this book independently, you would do well to set yourself a schedule of fifteen weeks and stick with it.

Your Reading Schedule

Number of books _____

Books you will read.

1. _____
2. _____

3. _____

4. _____

5. _____

6. _____

When and where can you do your daily reading?

_____

_____

Will you make one more agreement with yourself? Remember that writing is language, and any writer who gets anywhere has to be passionate about language. With that in mind, you will need to get in the habit of keeping your best dictionary *within an arm's reach* of where you read; and you need to look up *every* unfamiliar (or even slightly questionable) word you see. This is an important habit. And after you get used to it, it's fun. By signing your name below, you indicate your intention to establish this habit.

Signature _____

CLASS EXERCISE

My little reading list above is very abbreviated and incomplete. Class discussion can help you flesh out and customize your personal reading list. All members of the class, instructor included, should write down the name of the book that has most inspired them.

What was the book and why was it so influential?

_____

_____

_____

What did you learn from it about writing?

_____

_____

_____

SCRAPBOOK EXCERCISE

Start keeping records of readings in the scrapbook section of this book. These don't have to be analytical or critical. But it's good for you to write down thoughts, *any* thoughts, about what you are reading. You should soon get to the point where you wouldn't think of sitting down to read without a pen and paper handy, any more than you'd sit down to read without your dictionary nearby.

SUGGESTIONS FOR CURRENT PROJECT

Right now, all you need to do is to keep putting words on paper. Get comfortable with your own working rhythm. Make it a habit. When you get to the point where it's more trouble not to write than it is to write, you'll be making real progress. We'll be talking about technique soon enough; right now, just start generating the raw material, no matter how raw it might be.

ONE MORE WORD ABOUT BOOKS

Of course you can get books at the library, and you should. But you should also remember that if you are a serious writer, you are tying your fate to a struggling publishing industry that needs all the help it can get. When you buy books, especially hardcover originals (not cheap, I'm sorry to say), you are investing in yourself. And it's another way of *acting* like a writer. Real writers buy books.

3

Getting Focused

PURPOSE OF CHAPTER

The purpose of this chapter is to get you focused on your main writing project. Your project can be anything, as long as it's fiction. And please understand that *it doesn't have to be any good*.

Like the productions of a beginning violin player, your early work is likely to be bad, perhaps painfully bad. Don't worry about that; just write. If you can put up with being terrible for a while, you'll have a much better chance of becoming good.

And actually, as a writer, you are luckier than a violin player. Beginning fiction writers, even terrible ones, almost always come up with one or two interesting phrases, an unusual view of the world, a quirky and individual voice, something they can show their friends without embarrassment. The fledgling Pinchas Zuckerman must squeak and squawk for months, producing nothing of interest to anybody but a violin teacher. Consider yourself lucky.

CLASS EXERCISE

Here is another questionnaire. Fill it out as honestly as you can. Its purpose is to give you an idea of where you are starting from and what your strengths and weaknesses as a writer are.

If you are using this book independently, don't skip this exercise. These are questions you need to be thinking about—maybe even more so, because nobody's going to point out your problems for you.

A QUESTIONNAIRE ABOUT WHY YOU WRITE

1. Why are you in this class? (Or why are you working independently with this book?) Be honest. If you're here primarily to fulfill an academic requirement, don't be embarrassed to say so. Plenty of fine writers got started by accident.

   _____

   _____

2. What do you hope to accomplish?

   _____

   _____

3. What have you read that most made you want to be a writer?

   _____

   _____

4. Why did it affect you that way?

   _____

   _____

5. What have you read that most made you want to *quit* writing?

   _____

   _____

6. Why did it make you want to quit?

   _____

   _____

7. What is there about your life, your mind, your personality, that suggests to you that you can learn to write something interesting?

     _____

     _____

     _____

8. Describe the first project you want to work on. Is it a short story? Or do you want to start right off on a novel? (There's nothing wrong with starting off with a novel. It's a fallacy that you have to write short stories first.) If you don't know what you want to work on, this is as good a place as any to start thinking about it.

     _____

     _____

FIELD EXERCISE

Fiction is about problems. For the first field exercise, your instructor will dismiss the class for about fifteen minutes. Leave the classroom and begin discreetly observing people, in the classroom building or anywhere you can get to in a few minutes. Just *don't go to the library*. Libraries are good for many things, but they don't work for field exercises. Keep looking at people until you find somebody who seems to have a problem. Try to notice as many things about that person as you can, and try to understand the person's problem as well as you can. If some students wish to leave their possessions in the classroom during this field exercise, the instructor should stay behind to watch over purses, books, and coats.

Back in Class

Ask yourself: What was the problem?

_____

_____

What kind of a person was it who had the problem?

_____

_____

_____

How did this person react to the problem?

_____

_____

Has the person had this problem before? Explain.

_____

_____

Will the person have it again? Explain.

_____

_____

How do you think the problem will turn out?

_____

_____

What could happen to make it worse?

_____

_____

How does this problem resemble (or differ from) the problem that drives your project?

_____

_____

Do you know what your own protagonist's central problem is?

_____

_____

SCRAPBOOK EXERCISE

As you do your personal reading from your individual reading list, look for the problems that drive the stories. What is Huck Finn's problem? What is the problem facing the narrator of "Bartleby the Scrivener"? Learn to see fiction in terms of the problems; that will help you to conceive a story fully.

SUGGESTIONS FOR CURRENT PROJECT

Ask yourself if the problem in your own project is clear enough. If it's not, how could it be clearer? Are you being *cruel* enough to your characters? In other words, are you filling their existence with significant problems? And are the problems important enough—and interesting enough—to make a reader care about how, and if, they are resolved?

4

❖

Where Do Stories Come From?

PURPOSE OF CHAPTER

The purpose of this chapter is to "demystify" the process of telling stories, to show what a natural and instinctive thing it is to tell a story, and to help you see that stories aren't really all that complicated.

I heard a theory somewhere that fiction was invented concurrently with the campfire. I think I believe it. Before the campfire there would have been no focal point to human experience; but around the newly invented fire people could talk, brag, exaggerate. Probably as the cave people sat around telling their anecdotes of hunting skill and close calls with predators, somebody began sneaking in extra details. This would make him the first liar—a very important figure in human history.

Perhaps a sense of competition began to develop—something similar to what you hear when groups of people talk about their ailments: "You think that's bad? You should have seen what happened to my leg when the saber-tooth tiger bit me."

At some point this speaker's listeners must have stopped caring that he was a liar and simply let themselves enjoy his stories. This would make him the first entertainer. Starting with that moment around the campfire, it's not a long way to the traveling bard, or the spooky old lady who tells fairy tales, or to the tradition of fiction—word processors notwithstanding—that you yourself are involved in.

CLASS EXERCISE

If the campfire is the most natural way to tell stories, then the easiest way to generate stories in a classroom might be to recreate an imaginary campfire, within the limits of reason and fire safety.

For this exercise, students in the class will form their own groups of four or five. Sit in a circle, and just start telling stories. About what? Well, what did the cave people talk about? About their lives, for a start, their problems, worries, and triumphs. What was the best thing that happened to you in the last twenty-four hours? The worst thing? The funniest thing? The most frightening thing?

My theory is that the impulse of fiction grew out of the natural tendency of people to want to "top" other people's stories. In real life that's an annoying impulse; and you probably know people who are no fun to talk to because they always have to do you one better: if you went to Cleveland, they went to Tierra del Fuego. If you got stung by a bee, they got bitten by a tarantula.

In fiction, though, it's healthy to want to improve on what other people say. So as you go around the imaginary campfire circle, from anecdote to anecdote, see if you can convincingly improve on the story you heard before.

After ten or fifteen minutes of this, each group should choose the most interesting anecdote and compose a synopsis, consisting of not more than twenty words. Then a representative of each "campfire" group can read that group's synopsis, after which the class as a whole will choose the most interesting.

The last part of this exercise, which is derived from Pamela Painter and Anne Bernays's book *What If?*, consists of everybody in the class writing a series of twenty-five "What if?" questions, as a way of searching for the various directions this group anecdote can take. Just fill in the blanks in the form that follows—with anything, remembering that the act of asking these questions is just as important as their content. The instructor can ask students to read their favorite questions, but don't feel pressured into reading anything you think is embarrassingly dumb.

Synopsis of Chosen Group Anecdote

_____

_____

"What If" Questions

1. What if _____?
2. What if _____?
3. What if _____?
4. What if _____?
5. What if _____?
6. What if _____?
7. What if _____?
8. What if _____?
9. What if _____?
10. What if _____?
11. What if _____?
12. What if _____?
13. What if _____?
14. What if _____?
15. What if _____?
16. What if _____?
17. What if _____?
18. What if _____?
19. What if _____?
20. What if _____?
21. What if _____?
22. What if _____?
23. What if _____?
24. What if _____?
25. What if _____?

Why go through all this when it's not directly related to any of the stories the class is working on? The answer is that I'm trying to influence your behavior as much as your writing style. Writers compulsively ask "What if?" Writers hear stories and want to "top" them. Writers feel the impulse to dramatize their own lives, and the lives of their friends, even at the expense of accuracy. Developing those mental habits is just as important as developing the technical skills we'll be talking about later.

FIELD EXERCISE

What did the most interesting campfire ideas have in common? Almost certainly they had to do with *conflict*.

A story begins when somebody has a problem. Huckleberry Hound takes a job babysitting for a baby who keeps turning into a monster. An out-of-work schoolteacher has the bad luck to sign on to a whaling ship crew— under a mentally ill captain. A police chief must protect his town from a marauding shark—with little help from the shortsighted townspeople. Conflict. Problems, and not easily solved. This is what fiction is made of.

With that in mind, I'm going to send you out of the room again. This time your task is to eavesdrop, to find a place where you can unobtrusively listen to some conversations. Keep listening until you hear something conflict-ridden, something about a problem, a struggle, an argument. Chances are that you won't have to listen for long.

Again, it doesn't matter whether or not you end up doing anything with the material you are gathering. The point is to make yourself aware that the conflicts of real life are of a piece with the conflicts to be found in novels, short stories, plays, and movies.

A QUESTIONNAIRE ABOUT EAVESDROPPING

Who did you listen to?

_____

_____

_____

What were they talking about?

_____

_____

_____

What was the central problem they were talking about?

_____

_____

How would you characterize the problem (comic, tragic, mundane)?

_____

What kind of a work of fiction could be based on the conversation you listened to?

_____

_____

At the end of this field exercise, students should report to the class on what they have come up with. Don't worry if some of the conversations you heard were a little boring. If they took place in a school, they might have been about grades and academic issues. The point is not to come up with world-shaking plots, but to train yourself to see the conflicts that lie in the center of all dramatic occurrences.

SCRAPBOOK EXERCISE

Now that you've broken the ice about telling anecdotes in small groups, take some time at home to come up with a really well-organized short anecdote. A joke is permissible; just make sure that it's good and thoroughly prepared. Remember, you're being trained not just as a solitary writer, but as a social storyteller, so it's healthy for you to move from small groups, like the camp-fire circles, to larger groups, like the classroom. Learn to be a bit of a show-off; it's part of the writer's trade.

Depending on the size of the overall class, the instructor can have students tell their prepared anecdote to the whole class or to smaller "breakout" groups.

SUGGESTIONS FOR CURRENT PROJECT

Imagine that instead of writing your project you are telling it to your friends around a campfire. Ask yourself: what would you probably leave out? What would you add to? What would they like best? Where would they get bored?

You don't have to rework your project into a spoken monologue, but it's important to remember that even the most literary of works owes its existence to the ancient tradition of storytelling.

5

Creating Characters

PURPOSE OF CHAPTER

Fiction is about conflict, but conflict isn't interesting unless it involves people. The purpose of this chapter is to show you how character drives a story, and to help you get started putting together interesting and vivid characters.

How does character drive a story? What does that mean? Let me illustrate what I mean through a very simpleminded example. Watching the old *Superman* television show as a little kid, I realized early on that every episode was resolved the same way: by Superman's super powers. Superman uses his X-ray vision to melt the Kryptonite, Superman flies to the *Daily Planet* office in time to defuse the bomb. It was always the super powers. The story was never resolved by having Superman just do something clever, or by Jimmy Olson tricking the crooks.

Think about any TV show, cartoon, movie, short story, novel—anything fictional. One way or another, the action is propelled by the character. What would *Gone With the Wind* be without the fiery and indomitable spirit of Scarlett O'Hara? It would be a big, shapeless historical novel with no narrative center. Without the interplay of the characters' personalities, *The Great Gatsby* would be nothing but a sociological vignette.

It is the individual characters, even though they don't really exist, that make the fiction interesting. The American Revolution took place a long time ago, and everybody who fought in it is now dead. But there are many people alive today who learned more about the Revolution from the novel *Johnny Tremaine*, the story of a boy who never existed, than from their history classes.

I'm trying to go easy on the slogans, but here's one: *Character drives fiction*. Memorize it.

CLASS EXERCISE

Characters don't really exist, but to make up for that handicap they need to be vividly imagined. Here's an exercise to help you imagine characters. The instructor should cut at least ten faces out of various magazines, paste them onto a page, number them, and then photocopy the whole page for everybody in the class. Everybody in the class picks one of the faces to describe. Really describe that face; go beyond the usual superficialities.

Part of the fun of that exercise is the guessing game aspect: can you be the first person to identify which picture the person is talking about? Beyond that, however, see if you can train yourself to *really* see the complexity and subtlety of faces. What did your classmates notice about a face that you didn't—and what did you notice that nobody else did? Force yourself to keep describing these people even after you feel you've already said everything. That's when it gets interesting.

The second part of this exercise goes beyond mere description and asks you to speculate about what kind of people you are looking at. What are their lives like? What do they care about? What kind of a part would this person play—in what kind of a story?

After you've worked on these photocopied characters in class, choose two that you find most interesting. Cut their pictures out from the hand-out sheet and paste them in the space below, then answer the questions that follow.

```
┌─────────────────────────────┐
│                             │
│                             │
│                             │
│                             │
│   (Space for Character # 1) │
│                             │
│                             │
│                             │
│                             │
└─────────────────────────────┘
```

Character's name _____

Nickname _____

Age _____

Occupation _____

Religion _____

Most vivid physical characteristic

_____

Most vivid psychological characteristic

_____

What does this person want most?

_____

What does this person fear most?

_____

What kind of a story could this person play a part in?

_____

What kind of a part?

_____

_____

(Space for Character # 2)

Character's name _____

Nickname _____

Age _____

Occupation _____

Religion _____

Most vivid physical characteristic

_____

Most vivid psychological characteristic

_____

What does this person want most?

_____

What does this person fear most?

_____

What kind of a story could this person play a part in?

_____

What kind of a part?

_____

_____

FIELD EXERCISE

The whole point of this book is to get you thinking like a writer, to get you into the habit of observing people closely, and with an increased sensitivity to the possible complexity of their lives.

The next out-of-classroom exercise I'm going to ask you to do involves simply watching people until you see somebody who could become a fictional character. This has to be a stranger—no fair using your friends. Give this stranger a name, and identify the stranger's most vivid physical characteristic. Then decide what kind of a story this person could play a part in, and be prepared to report to the class on your observations and thoughts.

SCRAPBOOK EXERCISE

Keep watching people. Single out, and name, at least two strangers. Record their names and most important physical and emotional characteristics in the scrapbook section of this book. You've never met these people, but how do you feel about them? Are they positive or negative characters?

READING EXERCISE

What are you reading now? Just answer the questions below about your current main reading project.

Who is the main character?

_____

What is the most important thing about that character?

_____

_____

What does the character look like?

_____

_____

What is the character's emotional center?

_____

_____

How is this character different from anybody you've ever read about?

_____

_____

How does this character drive the story? In other words, what would happen if the main character were different?

_____

_____

How do you feel about the character? Is this character the kind of person you'd want to be friends with?

_____

_____

SUGGESTIONS FOR CURRENT PROJECT

The late John Gardner had a strict rule that *any* character in fiction, no matter how insignificant, must be rendered vividly. Keeping in mind Gardner's principle, as well as the questions we've been asking in this chapter about characters, go over as much of your current project as you can, and ask yourself if the characters are vivid enough. What could you do to make them more real?

This might not be the time to involve yourself in a major revision, especially since you need to establish some forward momentum in your work. But do be aware of where you need further development. Mark up your manuscript with remarks and suggestions for developing characters. That way you'll have something to work with when you get to the stage of serious revision.

6

Developing Characters

Purpose of Chapter

Chapter Five introduced the importance of character in fiction. But character is so important that it needs at least two chapters. In this chapter we'll go further into the idea of character driving fiction. We'll also talk about the difference between *flat* and *round* characters, as well as the difference between *static* and *dynamic* characters.

Flat and Round Characters

All characters need to be vividly rendered, but not all characters can be, or should be, rendered with the same complexity. That's why we make the distinction between a *flat* character (one dominated by a single characteristic) and a *round* character (a character complex enough to allow for internal contradiction). Notable exceptions to the rule exist, but we generally hope that our principal characters will have enough complications to achieve roundness, and we generally relegate our flat characters to the minor roles.

The clearest examples I can give of this idea are from a book I hope you've read. Huck, the half-educated ragamuffin who narrates Mark Twain's *Adventures of Huckleberry Finn*, certainly contains enough internal conflict and unpredictability to qualify as a fully-realized round character. Huck's brutal and alcoholic father, Pap Finn, is a flat character. This is not to say he's not interesting. Following Gardner's dictum, Pap is rendered with great vividness and clarity, managing to be at once funny and horrible. But his drunkenness and his brutality so dominate his portrait that he never gets rounded out—nor should he be.

STATIC AND DYNAMIC CHARACTERS

The greatest difference between cartoons and real stories, is that cartoon characters don't change—not even when they get shot in the face with a cannon. The indestructibility of Huckleberry Hound is comforting, somehow; but real life is about people changing, and the most interesting stories and novels almost always describe a significant change in a person's life. That's why it's helpful to make a distinction between *static* characters (those who don't change) and *dynamic* characters (who change, develop, or deteriorate during the course of the narrative).

Again, *Adventures of Huckleberry Finn* can furnish us with examples that I hope most readers will be familiar with. In the course of the narrative, Huck has changed greatly—beginning as an ignorant and superstitious youngster with little regard for other human beings, and ending up as an aware and sensitive person who sees people as individuals.

Tom Sawyer, reappearing from *The Adventures of Tom Sawyer*, the novel to which *Huck Finn* is a sequel, has changed little from the previous (and less interesting) book. Tom Sawyer remains a self-indulgent romantic, more interested in the adventure of rescuing Jim from slavery, than in the idea that a person's life is at stake. Although Huck goes along with Tom's plans, it's clear by the end of the book that Huck has become a man and that Tom remains a boy.

CLASS EXERCISE

Here are two character checklists similar to ones used in many fiction and drama classes. The first is designed for main characters; the shorter second one is for minor characters. You are welcome to make as many photocopies of these checklists as you need. The class may want to start out at first filling it out on the blackboard, using a familiar public figure or fictional character.

Later, as a class game, each student can secretly be given the name of a well-known historic or fictional figure, and then fill out this form and see if other students can tell who the student is talking about.

Finally, you can use copies of this checklist as many times as you want to help you construct the main characters for your own work. You'd better make the photocopies first, though, and leave the form in the book blank.

MAIN CHARACTER CHECKLIST

(Adapted from lists used at the University of Central Oklahoma)

Name _____

Nickname _____

Reason for name or nickname _____

_____

Physical Appearance

Age _____ Date of birth _____ Place _____

Hair color _____ Style _____

Eyes _____ Glasses? _____

Skin tone _____ Type _____

Shape of face _____

Facial hair/Makeup _____

Weight _____ Height _____ Build _____

Special physical characteristics _____

_____

_____

General health _____

Specific health problems _____

First thing you notice _____

What does character consider his or her best characteristic? _____

_____

Worst characteristic? _____

Preferences/Tastes

Favorite color _____

Favorite foods _____ Drinks _____

Music _____ Favorite song _____

Reading _____ Favorite movie _____

Leisure activity _____

Clothing _____ Work _____

Play or relaxation _____

Favorite article of clothing _____

Shoes _____

Jewelry _____

Smoker? _____ Smokes what? _____

Drives? _____ Drives what? _____

What kind of driver? _____

Lives (e.g., apt. house) Description _____

_____

Alone? Roommate? Family? _____

   Reasons _____

Pets? Description _____

Family and Personal Life

Married/single? _____ Previous marriages _____

_____

Straight/gay/bi? _____

Living with lover? _____

Name and age of spouse/lover _____

Happy/unhappy relationship? _____

Children _____

Outside relationships? _____

Previous romantic/sexual relationships _____

_____

_____

Childhood

Father's occupation _____

Mother's occupation _____

Relationship with character _____

_____

_____

Income group _____

Happy/broken/dysfunctional home? _____

Siblings _____

Names and ages _____

Relationship with character _____

Other significant family members living or dead

_____

_____

_____

Background and Personality

Religious upbringing _____

Present religious practice _____

Education _____

Career _____   Happy/unhappy? _____

Income _____

Future hopes/plans _____

_____

Fears _____

Worst problem _____

Special gifts or talents _____

_____

Good traits _____

_____

  Acknowledged? _____

Bad traits _____

_____

  Admitted? _____

Philosophy _____

_____

How is this character *changing*? _____

_____

_____

Friends: Same sex _____

         Opposite sex _____

Attitude toward money _____

Who most influenced character's life? _____

   Description _____

                  _____

                  _____

Who does character trust most? _____

   Least? _____

What doesn't this character understand? _____

_____

What is character's greatest regret? _____

_____

What is character most proud about? _____

_____

What are character's prejudices? _____

   Admitted? _____

Character's most valued possession _____

_____

Public figure character most admires _____

_____

What would character write on own gravestone? _____

_____

Minor Character Checklist

Character's name _____

Nickname _____

Reason for name or nickname _____

_____

_____

Age _____

Occupation _____

Religion _____

Most vivid physical characteristic _____

_____

Most vivid psychological characteristic _____

_____

What does this person want most? _____

_____

What does this person fear most? _____

_____

What would this character's theme music sound like? _____

_____

What kind of a story could this person play a part in? _____

_____

What kind of a part? _____

_____

FIELD EXERCISE

Here's another opportunity to observe people as *characters*.

All you have to do this time is find two strangers who can become characters. Look for one who can become a round character and one who can become a flat character. Give them names, then write down or remember as much as you can about them. Then return to class and go around the room, with each student giving a thumbnail sketch of the round and flat character.

SCRAPBOOK EXERCISE

Character is often defined by something small: a gesture, a look, an inappropriate smile. Learn to look for that defining trait that reveals a person. It always pops up sooner or later. A politician in the heat of a debate glances down impatiently at his watch; a young teacher yelling at a student lowers her eyes when he looks back at her.

In the scrapbook section, make a list of three people—friends, associates, adversaries—you know well. See if you can find the crucial expression, gesture, or mannerism that defines each of these familiar people.

This exercise is for your own benefit, so consider any classroom discussion of this section voluntary. Don't feel pressured to reveal anything that would embarrass or annoy your friends.

READING EXERCISE

Do the same with your current reading. List at least three characters from your reading projects, and write down the "telling" moment that defines each one. This won't always be easy. Maybe with some characters you'll never really find it. But you need to get in the habit of looking at how behavior defines a character. Remember that character isn't only a set of static attributes, like a wanted poster. It's most interesting when it's revealed by behavior.

SUGGESTIONS FOR CURRENT PROJECT

Make sure you leave the copy of the character checklist in the book blank, and do all your work from photocopies. You will want to use it later, to examine your own main character. For the time being, just make a list of all your characters, designate whether you think they are *flat* or *round* characters, *static* or *dynamic* characters. List also the *one* most important thing you know about each of these characters, and then list at least one way in which that character can become more real and more believable.

7

❖

Making Your Characters Talk

PURPOSE OF CHAPTER

"What is the use of a book," wonders Alice in the first scene of *Alice in Wonderland*, "without pictures or conversations?" Alice has a point. Although most serious fiction doesn't include pictures (some notable exceptions are John Gardner's *Freddy's Book* and Jack Finney's *Time and Again*), those "conversations" that Alice talks about are just about essential.

Good dialogue allows a writer to advance and explain elements of a story without having to resort to dull paragraphs of explanation that nobody is going to read. Dialogue allows characters to define themselves more memorably than could a whole page of authorial comments. Dialogue also makes prose easier on the eye, by breaking up paragraphs and "ventilating" the page.

Notice, for instance, how this passage of dialogue from William Kennedy's *Ironweed* succeeds in locating the novel in historical time (1938—the morning after Orson Welles's panic-inducing *War of the Worlds* broadcast) and at the same time illustrates both the befuddlement and the humor of the two bums who are talking about it.

From William Kennedy, *Ironweed* (New York: Viking Penguin, 1983):

"Hey, what the hell was all that about the man from Mars last night? Everybody was talkin' about it at the hospital. You hear about that stuff on the radio?"

"Oh yeah. They landed."

"Who?"

"The Martians."

"Where'd they land?"

"Someplace in Jersey."

"What happened?"

"They didn't like it no more'n I did."

Some avant-garde fiction gets by with little or no dialogue, but in general, if you want your work to be readable and interesting, you need to learn to write lively and believable dialogue.

It's not easy. You'll probably find that the hardest thing is making people sound like individual speakers. The one advantage you have, however, is that even if you haven't been reading or listening to good prose all your life, you have spent a lifetime listening to and participating in the most realistic dialogue imaginable.

In this chapter I'm going to give you a few hard-and-fast rules about dialogue. Dialogue is one of those areas where you *can* say "This is good and this is bad." Then I'm going to give you some exercises and practice drills that should help you develop some facility with writing dialogue.

SOME RULES ABOUT DIALOGUE

1. Don't write "Tom Swiftie" dialogue.

Tom Swift was the hero of a series of children's novels, and "Tom Swifties" were jokes modeled after the overwritten dialogue of those books, as in "I'd like to ride that pony," Tom said hoarsely; or "I think I'm going to die," Tom croaked.

Lines of dialogue do not benefit by fancy synonyms for "said," as in:

"Back off!" he challenged.

or: "What do you mean?" she flung back.

or: "I love carbonated drinks," Tom bubbled.

Let me tell you right now that "said" is one of the few words in the English language that never becomes monotonous. You can use it fifty times on a page if you need to.

And you don't need to explain how someone said something. ("Oh nuts!" he said angrily.) Let the character's words speak for themselves.

Beginning writers should use no word other than "said." Sure, pulp writers break this rule all the time, but they know what they're doing (sort of) and they're getting paid for it. You aren't. In general, it's much better if you let the actual speech carry the emotion, instead of tacking on the emotion to the attribution.

2. Don't be a tough guy.

"Hardboiled" dialogue, ("Buzz off, buster," I snapped, then went back to cleaning my snub-nosed police '38.) is just as lifeless as romance dialogue. And never refer to characters in dialogue by an article of clothing or a physical attribute. If someone wears a trench-coat, don't refer to that person as "Trenchcoat," as in:

> The boss's pinky ring twinkled as his trenchcoated henchman held the cowering prisoner.
>
> "You want I should whack him, boss?" insinuated Trenchcoat.
>
> "Nah," resolved Pinky Ring. "I'll do it myself."

3. Clarity above all.

Many contemporary writers don't use quotation marks in dialogue. I wouldn't recommend that a beginner dispense with quotes, but if you can drop the quotes and still retain the clarity, go ahead.

You also don't have to identify the speaker with every line. You only have to name the speaker often enough so that your reader will know who is talking. If your speakers sound very different from each other, you can go on as long as you like without any labels, as long as the reader doesn't risk getting lost.

Dialogue is often interspersed with action, and ideally this keeps the dialogue from becoming monotonous or mannered. But be careful. Thousands of detectives have lit countless cigarettes, all for the purpose of livening up dead dialogue, and all they have to show for it are overflowing ashtrays and ominous coughs. And make sure you avoid the worst cliché of all. Never say "He let a beat pass."

CLASS EXERCISE

For this exercise the instructor and the class need to come up with a dialogue situation in which two people are talking and each speaker wants something specific. Rather than dictating a situation, it might be useful to let the class make suggestions about what the situation is and what these characters' wants are. Then the students can work together in pairs, each one taking the part of one of the characters. One student will write one line in the voice of one of the characters, and then give the paper to the other student, who will write the other side of the dialogue.

It's important for the characters to want something specific. When each character has an agenda, dialogue has energy. Remember that gestures, actions, pauses (within reason), are part of dialogue. Each writer in each paired group should include the appropriate dialogue tags and accompanying actions (She said . . . . He looked away . . .).

FIELD EXERCISE

You don't want to go overboard and make either a nuisance or a fool of yourself—but it is important to keep making sorties out of class to observe and comment on the world and the people in it. And I think that doing it during class sessions, and wandering around under the auspices of an official class, helps to stress the idea that observing the world as a writer is serious business. It's more than a hobby, and more than something you do when you happen to think of it.

With those thoughts in mind, be prepared to do some more eavesdropping in any public place you can get to and back, either by foot, car, or public transportation, in about twenty minutes.

What you are looking for this time is dialogue. Listen as closely as you can, waiting for the strangest, funniest, or most interesting exchange of dialogue. Memorize as much of it as you can, and then write it down discreetly.

Back in class, students can read aloud the "found dialogue" passages they have come up with. The class can then choose the one with the most potential—and expanding it individually into a real passage of dialogue can become an in-class exercise.

SCRAPBOOK EXERCISE

See if you can extend this chapter's field exercise to your daily experience. Keep your small notebook handy and write down as many "found" dialogue passages as you can. The point is not so much that you're supposed to use them at some point, but that you're supposed to listen, and to get in the habit of hearing.

READING EXERCISE

As you continue with your current reading, I need to tell you about a paradox concerning "realistic" dialogue. I've been asking you to listen to real people talking, for the purpose of tuning your ear to spoken language. But that's only half the project. At the center of the study of dialogue is the paradoxical fact that "realistic" dialogue does not really exist. You might think that dialogue transcribed from real conversations would be gritty and believable, but it doesn't usually work that way. The most effective written dialogue sounds realistic but it isn't. It's foreshortened, tidied up. In other words, you won't get a handle on dialogue solely from listening to people talk (though you can't do without that; the best student dialogician I've ever worked with had grown up with seven brothers and sisters, resulting in a deeply ingrained feel for how people talk.) To make your dialogue really come alive, you also have to read good popular fiction, and to pay attention to the way characters talk.

Pay attention to these ideas as you continue reading. Where does "real life" realism end and fictional realism begin? In other words, what passages of dialogue can you find that wouldn't be natural in the real world but come off as natural in the real world of a book?

SUGGESTIONS FOR CURRENT PROJECT

The most important thing you can do with your current project is to keep your momentum up. So when these instructions ask you to backtrack, just do the thinking you need to, and make the supplementary notes you need, but don't stop moving forward with the main thrust of your project.

What you need to do right now with your project is to find a place where a narrative passage or a piece of explanation can be replaced by natural-sounding dialogue. If you have the time, write some of that dialogue; if not, just designate the passage to be rewritten later as dialogue.

And bear in mind that dialogue is a favor to your readers. It almost always makes prose more readable. Keep thinking about where dialogue passages will fit in your work.

8

❖

Making Things Happen

Purpose of Chapter

Why do people read fiction anyway? Life is short, and there's so much else to do. If I start reading a book, I'm making a rather large investment of time, energy, and money; and if I'm unable to care about a book, I'm likely to resent its author for wasting some hours or days of my life that I can't have back.

It might seem too obvious to say that what people care about in a story is what happens, how it develops, and how it turns out. But too many writers, especially well-educated and serious writers who ought to know better, try to get by on lyrical language, brilliant description, and intellectual monologue without actually having any real story to tell. Once in a while somebody gets away with a book like that, but the vast majority of plotless novels are artistic and commercial failures.

This chapter has been designed to help you understand what plot is, what it isn't, and how to get a handle on creating workable plots.

Let's take some simpleminded examples. Imagine that I'm telling you a story—of a happy family who get into their nice new car, and head across the country. At Niagara Falls they take a ride in the sightseeing boat. At Cleveland they spend a lovely day at the Cedar Point amusement park. In Chicago they visit the Grain Exchange, then continue west over the beautiful plains, which sparkle in the sunshine. Every song that comes on the car radio is a great song, and they all click their fingers in rhythm. On one perfect afternoon in Nebraska . . .

You don't like it? It's boring? How could it be boring? Wouldn't you like to take a relaxing trip like that? I would.

The reason this happy story is boring, of course, is that, although we might want our lives to be free of trouble and conflict, we need our stories to be about conflict. What else is there? Once there was a woman who was so poor that she had to sell her cow to buy food, but her son was such a jerk that he traded the cow for a handful of beans instead of money. Now there's trouble. What's going to happen? How's it going to turn out?

But plot isn't just what happens; plot is how it happens, how one thing leads inevitably to another. I like to watch Road Runner cartoons, but I know that they're not very strong on plot. The Coyote tries to chase the Road Runner with an Acme rocket. It instantly explodes, leaving Coyote charred. Coyote then sets up a system of ramps to roll a rock to crush Road Runner. Rock goes out of control, crushes Coyote down to a plate-sized figure who walks away with awkward little steps. Coyote then builds a fake railroad track to fool Road Runner, who runs right past, but when Coyote steps onto his track segment . . . of course the train runs him down.

Now this is all funny, and we wouldn't want these cartoons to be written any differently, but it doesn't really constitute a plot, because one thing doesn't build on another.

"Jack and the Beanstalk" is a familiar story with something more like a cause-and-effect plot. *Because* Jack's mother is so poor, she sends him to sell the cow. *Because* Jack is gullible, he accepts a handful of beans instead of money. *Because* of Jack's mistake, his mother throws the beans out the window. *Because* of throwing the beans, the beanstalk grows, and so on.

A plot needs two things. It needs a cause-and-effect structure, and it needs a central plot question. Two books that provide a good illustration of the difference between an episodic story and a story driven by a plot question are E.B. White's books *Stuart Little* and *Charlotte's Web*.

Stuart Little is a very enjoyable story, about a family whose son just happens to be a mouse. His adventures are very funny and exciting—but they are just that: a series of adventures without an overriding plot question to hold them together.

Compare that with *Charlotte's Web*. In that novel the plot question is clear, literally from the first sentence: "Where's Papa going with that axe?" Will Wilbur the pig live or die? That's what you call a clear and important plot question.

Here's a formula that comes from John Gardner's *On Becoming a Novelist*. This is Gardner's definition of every plot ever written:

> A central character wants something, goes after it despite opposition, perhaps including his own doubts, and so arrives at a win, lose or draw.

There's one more thing that's important. The ultimate plot is driven by character, not just by accident. Think of *Moby-Dick*. It's an accident that Ishmael and Queequeg sign up on a whaling ship captained by a psychotic, but it's the character of that psychotic Ahab that makes his mad chase at least somewhat believable.

You can see the character-driven structure particularly clearly in Tom Wolfe's *The Bonfire of the Vanities*, a masterfully plotted novel in which the main character's arrogance and fecklessness bring down a whole host of disasters on his head. *Because* he's the type of husband who has no qualms about having an affair with another woman, he ends up getting lost in his Mercedes in the middle of the South Bronx and injuring a kid. *Because* he's too much of a wimp to take responsibility for his own actions, he tries to get away with it, making things look much worse when he finally does get caught. *Because* he's overconfident and self-centered, he mounts a disorganized and ineffective defense.

Let me call your attention to one more important element in a good plot: the element of simplicity. I think that the essence of any good story can be stated in one sentence. So you should be wary if it takes you half a page to explain what your own story is about. Maybe you're not separating the essential from the unessential—or maybe you just have something impossibly cumbersome.

Look at the movie listings in *TV Guide*. It's amazing how clearly they can capture the sense and the spirit of a movie in ten or fifteen words: "*Captain Poopdeck*: Waterlogged swashbuckler about pirate (Charles Laughton) forced to bring his mischievous daughter (Shirley Temple) along on a voyage." "*Cut to the Chase*: A vacationing Don Johnson is up to his designer stubble in danger when he accidentally walks off with a million dollars in Colombian drug-lord money."

Can you do that for your own project? Can you catch the heart of it in twenty words? You should be able to. Remember that if you ever have a book published you will be asked to describe it in a short sound-bite, and it needs to be absolutely clear.

CLASS EXERCISE

For this exercise, students in the class should pair off at random. On a sheet of paper, each will write down a *plot need*. This should involve a central character, and it should be an important and somehow difficult goal (not something like needing to get to the mailbox to mail a letter). It doesn't have to be complicated; think of *Charlotte's Web*, a novel driven by Wilbur's simple wish to survive.

When both of you in the pair have formulated your own plot needs, you should trade papers and read what your partner has put down as a plot need.

Your job now is to *frustrate* your partner's need. What obstacle can you think of that will derail your partner's quest? Think of the story of Cinderella. The original plot need is for Cinderella to get to the ball, and by extension to escape from her squalid existence. And what could be a better primary obstacle than those cruel stepsisters?

No fair cheating. Give your partner a difficult obstacle, but not an insurmountable or catastrophic one. If your partner's plot need was for the character to become a Hollywood movie star, it would defeat the spirit of this exercise to have that character die in a plane crash before even getting there.

After you formulate your obstacle to your partner's plot need, trade papers again. Look at the obstacle you've been given. Then decide how to deal with it. What new measures can your protagonist take? Write them down, then trade papers again. Keep this up. For every new measure the protagonist resorts to, the antagonist will invent a way in which it can backfire. For each obstacle, the protagonist will think of a new strategy.

Keep trading papers like this until you have written in your original paper at least eight times. Then read them aloud in class, if you choose. Let the class judge if your exercise sounds like a real plot, and if it comes to some conclusion.

Don't worry if what you and your partner come up with sounds idiotic. The purpose of this exercise is not to devise workable plots on the spot, but to help you understand the dynamic of action/obstacle that is the heart of all plots.

FIELD EXERCISE

Keep thinking about that plot need. Then leave the class for fifteen minutes or so, and look around until you see someone with an apparent need. Observe that person as closely as discretion allows. Then fill out the form on the next page and report to class.

Field Report on Plot Need

Description of person observed

_____

_____

Where and when?

_____

_____

Doing what?

_____

_____

What do you think that person's plot need was?

_____

_____

_____

What makes you think so?

_____

_____

What do you think is this person's principal antagonist? (This doesn't have to be a person; it can be any force or circumstance standing in this person's way.)

_____

_____

What other possible ways can this person's need be frustrated?

_____

_____

How might this person's need be fulfilled?

_____

_____

READING EXERCISE

How does what we have been talking about square with what you see in your reading? Are you finding episodic structures, or do you see one development leading to another?

To keep you on your toes, fill out the questionnaire on the next page.

A PLOT QUESTIONNAIRE FOR CURRENT READING

Current book or story you are reading

_____

Main plot need

_____

Main obstacle

_____

Is the plot *episodic* (like *Stuart Little*) or *interconnected* (like *Charlotte's Web*)?

_____

In what way is that plot driven by character?

_____

_____

How do the main character's actions deepen the plot?

_____

_____

What is the most recent plot development at the point where you are in the book or story?

_____

_____

How did earlier events in the story lead up to this current development?

_____

_____

Do you see a climax coming?

_____

What might it consist of?

_____

SCRAPBOOK EXERCISE

Do you have a copy of *TV Guide* handy? If not, get one, and keep it around. It doesn't matter whether you watch the movies or not, but it is essential that you get in the habit of seeing the essence of a story.

Now think of your three favorite books. Write a fifteen to twenty word description of each, in the style of *TV Guide*, catching the gist and the spirit of the story. This might work as a game in class—to see who can be the first to guess which familiar story is being described.

SUGGESTIONS FOR CURRENT PROJECT

This would be a good time to review the plot elements of your project. The next page contains a questionnaire about your current plot developments. Fill it out as completely as you can. If you have to leave something out, don't worry about it—but do ask yourself the question: If this story lacks some important conventional plot element, what does it have that can make up for that lack?

You'll also have a place to write your own *TV Guide* blurb for your project.

A Plot Questionnaire
for Your Current Writing Project

Working title

_____

Main plot need

_____

_____

Main obstacle

_____

_____

In what way is the plot driven by character?

_____

_____

How do the main character's actions deepen the plot?

_____

_____

What is the most recent plot development at the point where you are in the book or story?

_____

_____

How did earlier events in the story lead up to this current development?

_____

Write your own *TV Guide* blurb. Make it as short and snappy as you can. Remember that this is largely a psychological exercise, and that the more clearly you can conceive of your project the more confidence you'll have in your writing.

_____

_____

_____

9

❖

Getting the Details Right

PURPOSE OF CHAPTER

Sometimes you'll be reading something and an image will jump off the page with such vividness that the whole story will come clear. John Updike will describe a girl being hassled by a store manager for coming into his store in a bathing suit, as a young employee watching comments that she "blushes, though maybe it's just a brush of sunburn I was noticing for the first time, now that she was so close."

Sometimes you'll be writing and an image will jump on to the page and you'll realize you've hit it just right. When that happens, you might feel a tingle of pleasure run up your spine. Writers have been feeling that for thousands of years. When it happens to you you'll understand that this is what it's all about.

The most vivid moments in literature are great because of the specific details the author puts in. The difference between Robert James Waller's generic Iowa landscape and Willa Cather's rich and fecund prairies, between a standardized Harlequin love scene and the pained eroticism of Nabokov's *Lolita*, is the difference between general description and specific detail.

Good fiction is specific. It is rich with details from all senses. It prefers the concrete to the abstract.

Describing a predatory drug addict in "How I Contemplated the World From the Detroit House of Correction and Began my Life Over Again," Joyce Carol Oates doesn't merely state the facts about how nasty this guy is. Instead she makes him real, saying, "His face is bony and cautions, the bones of his cheeks prominent as if with the rigidity of his ceaseless thinking, plotting, for he has to make money out of girls to whom money means nothing, they're so far gone they can hardly count it."

You've probably already heard the slogan, "Show, don't tell." It's already a cliché, but clichés become clichés because they're so true.

Good writers dramatize and illustrate. Dull writers explain. Consider this passage:

> 1.   I stood there thinking about how lonely I was, now that Susan had left me. What a terrible time it was for this breakup to happen, just when we were both at our most sensitive point, both emotionally and financially. If she had had a little more patience, we could have worked this out, or at least we could have ended it in a way that didn't leave us both in such a lonely and vulnerable position. We had made such a good couple, with so many things in common and such good chemistry between us. But I guess she needed something that I couldn't give her, which was very unfortunate, because now I needed something that I couldn't give myself either.

Now look at this one for comparison:

> 2.   I stood there by the steps that come out of the subway station in Columbus Circle, watching the taxis circle in a rush of yellow, and above them the pigeons in their steely shades of gray going around and around in the same direction, and above them a sky so flat you couldn't see if it was ten miles overhead or ten feet. It was rush hour. Everybody was going home, in their good shoes, some carrying leather briefcases whose shiny surfaces caught the green light of the fluorescent PIZZA sign across the street. They must have thought I was lost, standing and staring at their faces. What trick of mathematics is it that lets there be so many millions of faces, and not one of them recognizable?

What's the difference between these two paragraphs, both exploring similar moments of desolation? Paragraph 1 contains more information about how the speaker feels and what the speaker thinks. But it's *expository*; it explains rather than illustrates. It talks *about* feelings, but it doesn't let the reader *experience* any of the feelings.

Paragraph 2 contains far less explanation of the speaker's thoughts. It doesn't come right out and say how the narrator feels. But look at the things the narrator notices, the specific images he shares with the reader. Doesn't that moment have more emotional intensity than Paragraph 1?

CLASS EXERCISE

Start from where you are. Force yourself, right in class, to start noticing things. Do a ten minute in-class observation exercise with the following rules: look around the classroom until you notice something you've never noticed before. Then write it down. It doesn't matter if it's something trivial, like a sloppy paint job around the windows. The point of this exercise is to get you in the habit of noticing things.

Write down at least five things that you've noticed for the first time, *and that you will continue to notice from now on*. Decide which is the most important and which is the least important, and read those two to the class.

Another exercise that may help you learn to pay attention to details is to describe something that should be very familiar to you: the face of your watch (don't look), the steering wheel of your car, the shoes you have on, your front door. Describe one of these things as clearly as you can, then check yourself on how accurate you were. Remember that these are behavioral exercises as much as aesthetic ones. Writers notice details, often bizarre and irrelevant details. It's that habit of noticing that makes the difference between living prose and dead prose.

FIELD EXERCISE

If you could notice as much as you did cooped up in the classroom, imagine how much you can notice on the outside. This moment, in which you are out wandering around in the world but on a specific class assignment, is an important one for a writer. Find the most important thing you've never noticed before *and will always notice again from now on*, and bring it back to class.

SCRAPBOOK EXERCISE

This exercise asks you to take what you did in class and apply it to a number of familiar things. The form includes lists of "Things I never noticed about . . .

a certain person.   this town.
my house.   my favorite song.
somebody's car.   some celebrity.
school.

READING EXERCISE

This should be an easy one. Just keep reading, and be on the lookout for descriptive passages in which your author gets it *just right*—in which the author captures some element of reality with surprising vividness. Copy down at least three examples and bring them into class. Be prepared to fill in a little context and to discuss why you find the descriptions so apt.

SUGGESTIONS FOR CURRENT PROJECT

Look around in your project for a descriptive sentence that you think is dull and humdrum. Now force yourself to write ten sentences in the place of the first dull one. Keep going; keep looking for new details: *any* details. Don't worry; you don't have to leave any of this in—but don't delete it for twenty-four hours.

The point of this exercise is to help you learn to keep looking for details, for that one image that will make a person, place, or thing come alive. Try this exercise on at least three sentences in your writing, and then bring it to class. See what people in the class think of the difference between your one sentence and your ten sentences.

ONE LAST NOTE ABOUT DESCRIPTION

Be careful. Once you get good at writing description, there's a danger that it can get too easy and that you can overdo it. Nothing is more annoying than self-indulgent description that illustrates only its author's ego.

Look at the best fiction, how descriptive passages are always in some sort of context. Just keep it under control. Intersperse description with action and dialogue. Remember that description is the first thing that readers skip.

10

❖

The World of Your Story

PURPOSE OF CHAPTER

Every story or novel takes place somewhere. That somewhere can be a real place, like the New York of James Baldwin's "Sonny's Blues." It can be a fictional place, like William Faulkner's Yoknapatawpha County, Mississippi. Or it can be a place without a name, like the setting of William Gass's "In the Heart of the Heart of the Country."

Sometimes a story or a novel contains more than one of those things. Most of Fitzgerald's *The Great Gatsby* takes place in the fictional towns of East Egg and West Egg, but other chapters bring the narrator into the very real New York.

What all these settings must have in common is that they must be vivid. Whether they exist or not, the reader must be able to get a feel for them. I don't know what town in Indiana William Gass used as a model for "In the Heart of the Heart of the Country," but I know what the place looks like and feels like. I can never go to Yoknapatawpha County, because there's no such place on the map, but for any reader it is quite recognizable. In some of his editions Faulkner even provided a map and some demographic data. New York has changed a lot since the time when "Sonny's Blues" takes place, but I have no doubt about where I am as I ride in a taxi with Baldwin's narrator and his brother Sonny up Central Park West, "past the stony elegance of hotels and apartment buildings."

The purpose of this chapter is to help you understand the importance of setting, and to help you learn to locate your fiction in real or imagined places that will make the world of your story more real.

The Most Arbitrary Rule in this Book

Never use your own home town as a setting for your fiction.

It has been my experience that no story set in a student writer's home town is ever any good. This is true, I think, beause writers who use their home towns give up the opportunity to make an important fictional leap. By limiting their imaginations geographically, they tend to limit them in other ways.

I'm not saying you can't draw on real experiences and real places; I'm just saying they have to be fictionalized. Usually this is easy. Just change Denver to Albuquerque, Cleveland to Philadelphia. Use the road atlas to bring in realistic details. Remember, you're writing fiction. Tell as many lies as you can get away with.

You'll notice that accomplished writers break this rule all the time. You can break it too, once you understand how to use a real place as a spur to the imagination, rather than as a substitute for the imagination. For now, fictionalize your settings.

Class Exercise

For this exercise the class (or a handful of interested friends) will invent a place. Just go around the room, with each class member describing one characteristic of the place: name, population, climate, industry, architecture, history, demographics. What you come up with might seem a bizarre and contradictory place, but at least it will be a place, not just the vague background for a vague story.

As soon as this place has been fully described, everybody in the class will write the first paragraph of a story or novel set there. Then read them aloud. How has the setting influenced the kind of stories that seem to be shaping up?

Field Exercise

This field exercise is about finding the essence of a place. In the break period agreed upon, go as far from the class as you can, to someplace you have some feelings about, either positive or negative.

Now examine this place. Look at it. Listen to it. Smell it. Experience it in as many ways as you can. And then see if you can tell yourself what the essence of the place is. What is the heart of it? What makes it itself?

When you have come up with something, bring it back to the classroom and tell the class what you found. It should be encouraging to hear the diversity of places and impressions available even to beginning writers.

SCRAPBOOK EXERCISE

Make a list of several places that are personally important to you. Say what you think their essence is. Describe how you think those places could be altered so as to become a good fictional setting. Discuss the kinds of stories that could most easily take place in each of these places.

READING EXERCISE

As you continue through your current reading, ask yourself about the world in which the story takes place. Is it a real place, a fictional place, an unnamed place, or a combination of two or more of those things? Is it rendered in great detail, or by means of just a few key attributes? Does the place influence the story greatly, or is it a mere background?

SUGGESTIONS FOR CURRENT PROJECT

Go back through your own project, while thinking about settings. Where could your "world" have been more fully realized? What sort of locations would your readers be most curious about? Where have you failed to fictionalize it?

Don't spend too much time rewriting just now. Just make notes about what to expand, so you'll find them when you revise.

11

❖

Whose Story Is It?
Understanding Point of View

PURPOSE OF CHAPTER

Stories don't just appear: they are told—either by a character within the story or by a voice from outside the story. The various places in and out of the story where the author can situate the narration are what we mean when we talk about *point of view*, sometimes shortened to P.O.V.

Every story is told from some point of view. The purpose of this chapter is to make sure you know which is which, to help you gain some facility in using all the points of view available to you, and to help you decide which points of view you want to use for which purposes.

To run through it quickly, the most common points of view are *first person* (in which the narrator is an "I" who exists as a character in the story) and *third person* (in which the characters are referred to as "he" and "she" and the narrator doesn't have any personal existence).

When you tell something that happened to you, you use the *first person*. Narratives that need to get deeply into the mind of a character, like Marilynne Robinson's *Housekeeping*, or this passage from *The Catcher in the Rye*, often benefit from that technique.

Usually I like riding on trains, especially at night, with the lights on and the windows so black, and one of those guys coming up the aisle selling coffee and sandwiches and magazines. I usually buy a ham sandwich and about four magazines. If I'm on a train at night, I can usually even read one of those dumb stories in a magazine without puking. You know. One of those stories with a lot of phoney, lean-jawed guys named David in it, and a lot of phoney girls named Linda or Marcia that are always lighting all the goddam Davids' pipes for them. I can even read one of those lousy stories on a train at night, usually. But this time it was different. I just didn't feel like it. I just sort of sat and did nothing.

Now that's some personal information that would be hard to present convincingly from any other viewpoint.

Usually the "I" narrator of a first person story is the main character, but not always. In *The Great Gatsby*, the main characters are seen through the eyes of Nick Carroway, a minor player whose intelligence and open-mindedness give his vision a clarity that the major characters in the story could never achieve.

Usually the "I" narrator can be trusted to present the story clearly, but there are some distinguished exceptions. The neurotic and delusional housekeeper who narrates Henry James's *Turn of the Screw* is one of literature's most famous *unreliable narrators*. William Faulkner carried this idea to a high level when he told the first section of *The Sound and the Fury* through the voice of an idiot.

Jason threw into the fire. It hissed, uncurled, turning black. Then it was grey. Then it was gone. Caddy and Father and Jason were in Mother's chair. Jason's eyes were puffed shut and his mouth moved, like tasting. Caddy's head was on Father's shoulder. Her hair was like fire, and little points of fire were in her eyes, and I went and Father lifted me into the chair too, and Caddy held me. She smelled like trees.

The *third person* steps back from the action. In fiction it is seen as more objective, perhaps more scientific.

Third person narration can be classified into three types:

1. It can be *omniscient*, able to hear the thoughts of all characters at once, as in this passage from Harriet Beecher Stowe's *Uncle Tom's Cabin*.

Eliza stood for a moment contemplating this unfavorable aspect of things, which she saw at once must prevent the usual ferry-boat from running, and then turned into a small public house on the bank, to make a few inquiries.

The hostess, who was busy in various fizzing and stewing operations over the fire, preparatory to the evening meal, stopped, with a fork in her hand, as Eliza's sweet and plaintive voice arrested her. . . .

"I've got a child that's very dangerous," said Eliza. . . .

"Well, now, that's onlucky *[sic]*," said the woman, whose motherly sympathies were much aroused . . . .

2. Many stories use the *third person limited* point of view, meaning that the narrator can hear the thoughts of one character but not everybody in the story. Usually the limited narration focuses on the actions and thoughts of one main character, as in this section from the story "Paul's Case" by Willa Cather.

> When Paul went down to dinner the music of the orchestra came floating up the elevator shaft to greet him. His head whirled as he stepped into the thronged corridor, and he sank back into one of the chairs against the wall to get his breath. The lights, the chatter, the perfumes, the bewildering medley of color—he had, for a moment, the feeling of not being able to stand it.

3. The most uninvolved narrator is known as the *fly on the wall narrator* or *objective* narrator. This narrator makes no comment about the action, and reports nothing of what any characters think and feel, seeing and hearing only what a fly on the wall would notice. Hemingway took this technique to an advanced level in scenes like this one from the short story "Hills Like White Elephants."

> The woman brought two glasses of beer and two felt pads. She put the felt pads and the beer glasses on the table and looked at the man and the girl. The girl was looking off at the line of hills. They were white in the sun and the country was brown and dry.
>
> "They look like white elephants," she said.
>
> "I've never seen one," the man drank his beer.

4. You don't see it much, but there is such a thing as *second person* narration, in which the narrative voice addresses the main character as "you." It was used recently in Jay McInerny's *Bright Lights, Big City*. (New York: Vintage Books, 1987).

> At one o'clock you go out for a sandwich. Megan asks you to bring her a Tab. Downstairs you semi-revolve through the doors and think about how nice it would be not to have to return at all, ever. You also think about how nice it would be to hole up in the nearest bar. The glare from the sidewalk stuns you; you fumble in your jacket pocket for your shades. Sensitive eyes, you tell people.

What you need to do in this chapter is experiment with all the possible points of view, so that you will be comfortable using them. We'll go through several exercises in which you change points of view. The point here is not to influence your preferences (many writers settle eventually into a favorite method), only to help you be aware of the range of options.

CLASS EXERCISE

Now that you know the basic points of view, take a look at the illustration below. From how many viewpoints can it be described? Let everybody in the class pick one viewpoint, so that each character in the picture is represented by at least one class member.

Remember that writing from a certain individual's viewpoint doesn't mean that you have to limit yourself to the first person. You can explore a character's experience using the third person limited, and you can also look at the scene through an omniscient or objective narration.

After you have written your individual "take" on this scene, everybody in the class should read their passages aloud. Then, everybody should switch viewpoints and write a few lines from the point of view of a different character.

FIELD EXERCISE

By now you should have found some ways to observe people without making them nervous. The assignment this time is to observe a person in the outside world, determine what that person's primary need and primary antagonist are, and then to come back to class and write two separate passages about this person—one in the first person and one in the third person. When you read these aloud in class, and when you listen to other people in the class read their passages, think about how point of view affects the narration. Which characters work better in the third person? Listen to people in the class as they read. Do they seem more comfortable with one point of view than with another?

SCRAPBOOK EXERCISE

This will be a self-evaluation exercise. Every writer has a favorite point of view. What's yours? Is it working for you? Do you need to be more adventurous, or are you working in a form that succeeds for you?

A POINT OF VIEW QUESTIONNAIRE

1. What point of view have you felt most comfortable with?

   _____

   _____

2. In what way does that point of view work well for you?

   _____

   _____

3. Have you tried writing the same scene from alternate points of view?

   _____

   _____

4. Is there a point of view that you have avoided (or felt you failed with)?

   _____

   _____

READING EXERCISE

Take an inventory of your favorite novels and short stories. How are they told? Is there a pattern to the kind of narration you prefer to read, or do you pick and choose?

A READING QUESTIONNAIRE

Favorite Novels

1. _____ P.O.V. _____

2. _____ P.O.V. _____

3. _____ P.O.V. _____

4. _____ P.O.V. _____

5. _____ P.O.V. _____

Favorite Short Stories

1. _____ P.O.V. _____

2. _____ P.O.V. _____

3. _____ P.O.V. _____

4. _____ P.O.V. _____

5. _____ P.O.V. _____

SUGGESTIONS FOR CURRENT PROJECT

Take a look at what you are working on. As you go through this question-naire, think about how you chose your working point of view, and how well it's working.

A CURRENT PROJECT QUESTIONNAIRE

1. What point of view are you using?

   _____

2. Are you consistent with it, or do you change from section to section? (Changing is okay, as long as you're in control.)

   _____   _____

3. Have you tried other points of view? Which ones?

   _____

4. What is the chief benefit that your story derives from being told the way it is?

   _____

   _____

5. What handicap does your chosen point of view entail?

   _____

   _____

12

❖

How Not to Be Bad

PURPOSE OF CHAPTER

This is where we talk about the difference between being good and being rotten. My theory is that it is much more natural for a writer to be rotten than to be good. After all, the kind of vices that make for bad writing—sentimentality, dishonesty, frigidity, laziness, vagueness, and pop-sensibility—are endemic in every known society. I will discuss each of those vices as they apply to fiction later in this chapter. The virtues that make for good writing—patience, sensitivity, compassion, originality, courage—are best cultivated in solitude, and over time. You may take years to develop them. You may never really succeed.

And here we come to a sticky issue. All over the world, serious writers languish in poverty, while the writers of some miserable tripe have become millionaires.

Does that mean it's a waste of time to be a serious writer? I don't think so. The difference is not so much in the quality as in the aim. Serious fiction, like serious music or serious painting, is undertaken for the purpose of making the world more real, more interesting, and more available through language, and expanding the audience's experience by showing them something they've never seen before. Pop fiction aims to do pretty much the same thing again and again. That's why whole pop fiction genres have arisen: because one Gothic romance was such a success, dozens of writers soon realized that they could make money cranking out a similar product.

I don't want to be too high-toned about this, especially when you consider that much pop writing—like Mickey Spillane, Sue Grafton, Stephen King—is brilliantly done, and deserves to be read and admired.

And it's not a moral issue, either. The pop authors whose books you will see every time you go into a bookstore, with their latest bestseller piled in tall pyramids, are not slobs or fools or dilettantes. They're professionals, and besides, they're good for the economy. We need them to keep the book business going.

So if you think you have the stuff to be a pop author, I'll give you all the encouragement I can. I'll also tell you that there are many books on writing pop fiction that are more specialized and detailed than this one.

But if you want to write something that makes the world a more interesting place and makes people think something they haven't thought before (a wonderful ambition, even if you don't get a million dollars for it), here are some vices to watch out for.

THINGS BAD WRITERS DO

Sentimentality.   All writing is about emotion, and all good writing will in places emotionally move us. Consider this passage at the end of Nabokov's *Lolita*, when the narrator recalls a moment shortly after his child-mistress had been taken from him.

> And soon I realized that all these sounds were of one nature, that no other sound but these came from the streets of the transparent town, with the women at home and the men away. Reader! What I heard was but the melody of children at play, nothing but that . . . . I stood listening to that musical vibration from my lofty slope, to those flashes of separate cries with a kind of demure murmur for background, and then I knew that the hopelessly poignant thing was not Lolita's absence from my side, but the absence of her voice from that concord.

The tenderness and emotional intensity there is unmistakable, and there's also something else going on. That passage doesn't try to sound like anything else. It achieves its effect through its clarity and originality. For comparison, here is the same passage rewritten in a tear-jerking style:

> I stood there with my heart breaking in two, the clarity of her lost laughter still ringing in my ears, and the memory of all the songs we had sung together when our hearts were young echoing inside the emptiness of my lonely life like

a memory from the past. Far away I could hear the laughter of little children at play. One of them was carrying a teddy bear just like the one I had given her— oh, it seemed like a thousand years ago, back in that lost time when we had lived and loved together, our hearts beating together as one.

This is an extreme example of course, but you can find subtler examples of this kind of writing everywhere.

What happens in sentimentality is that the author takes a shortcut. Instead of coming up with something original to care about, or at least an original way to talk about it, the author uses a formula: a dead puppy, a lost love, and tries to make the *formula*, rather than the language, do all the work.

Sentimentality isn't just about tenderness, though. In *On Becoming a Novelist*, John Gardner rightly identified another tendency of the contemporary sentimentalist. If bogus tenderness and unearned innocence can be defined as a "Pollyanna" view of the world, the converse of that view—an equally unearned cynicism and a counterfeit grittiness—is just as sentimental in its own way. Gardner calls it "Dis-Pollyanna."

This last viewpoint, along with its usual "pop-grunge" setting of student slums and overflowing ashtrays, is tempting for the writer who wants to write something that sounds like the real world. There's nothing wrong with writing gritty fiction—it's just that too often the trappings take the place of the real story.

The thing about sentimentality, of both kinds, is that it simplifies life. Some readers want that, and that's why some dull writers get rich simplifying (and in the process impoverishing) the world. Real fiction enriches and celebrates the world by looking at it in all its complexity.

Frigidity.   Your characters aren't real, but they need to be treated with a certain compassion. When they aren't, when the author tries to show off and in the process makes the character do something unnatural or grotesque, we call that passage (and the writer if this becomes a habit) frigid. You can usually tell frigidity when you read it, because it gives you a particularly cold feeling in your stomach as you toss the book away. Here's an example.

> The Farnsworth children wouldn't be coming to Billy's birthday party today, because last night when their house burned down, they all became life-sized birthday candles. How inconvenient it would have been for them, metamorphosed in their peculiarly post-infernological manner, to have tried to play Pin the Tail on the Donkey with no hands to hold the tail with.

The reason a passage like that is so bad is that any legitimate reactions to the story—horror, sorrow, or even grim humor—take a back seat to the author's self-aggrandizing need to be clever.

Axe-grinding.   Stories are about what happens to people. They're only tangentially about ideas. When a writer uses a story to advance a particular idea, the story becomes didactic (and it doesn't help the idea much). When the hero of Christopher Zenowich's *The Cost of Living* visits a sales convention and gets depressed by the sight of "an entire convention center filled with proven methods of lifting money from consumer pockets into the corporate till," the author is grinding an axe rather than telling a story. This is not to say that social and political issues don't belong in fiction, or that you can't get subtle digs in against people and things you don't like. But the story has to come first.

Pop Sensibility.   Nobody wants to seem dated, but writers who try to be contemporary at the expense of taste and clarity, and especially writers who stick too many brand names into their fiction, cheapen the very thing they purport to be trying to enrich. Don't be too cool. Every writer has moments of feeling like a geek, and it's natural to want to compensate and to show the world that you're up on things. Just don't let it become a pose.

Dullness.   I don't want to make too much of these vices that I've been talking about, because they're not usually the real problem. The real problem— the mother of all literary vices—is *dullness*, and dull writing comes from a vague and dim view of the world. Truly bad writing—not just hack writing, which we may resent, but empty and dishonest writing, which we deplore— is dim. It doesn't see anything. It doesn't perceive the world; it doesn't make the reader perceive anything.

A truly dull writer would take the Nabokov passage we looked at earlier and turn it into something like this:

> I stood there thinking, listening to the pleasant sounds coming up from below, looking at the little community below me. That's when I realized that life can sometimes be very sad, and that I really didn't have much of a future. I could see the youngsters playing, and I could see that they were truly enjoying themselves, but that just made me more aware of how lonely I was in comparison, up there in the beautiful landscape, all alone.

What's wrong here is that there's nothing to grab onto, nothing to feel anything about. This is worse than bad; it's empty.

Class Exercise

I don't usually approve of being bad on purpose, but I'll have you do it here for a bit. In this exercise the class will write together, going through a sequence of stylistic voices. Keep as much as you can to the basic story that has been started here, but feel free to go off on your own stylistic tangents.

Start this way: First choose a setting, or a basic story. Then have everybody in the class write the first paragraph of that story in a "Pollyanna" voice, a voice of sweetness and light and refusal to look into the complexity and potential darkness of human existence.

For the next paragraph, everybody switch to the "Show-off" voice. Here it doesn't matter if the story holds together or if things make sense. All that matters is that you show how clever you are.

Now, take a paragraph to "grind your axe." What idea do you genuinely believe in—and who do you truly hate? Put this paragraph at the complete and abject service of that belief, and don't worry about quality.

The next stage is "pop sensibility." Show your audience how much you think you understand what's hot and what's not. Show how trendy you can be, and identify everything by its brand name. (If you want to write pop novels, this is a good thing to practice, because many successful pop novels have been described as being largely about brand names.)

Next, "Dis-Pollyanna." Show in this paragraph how tough and cynical you can be about the world, writing in a voice of bitterness and darkness, refusing to acknowledge any possibility of joy or redemption.

And finish the story with the worst vice of all: dimness. Tell the story, but don't get very far into it. Don't go beyond predictable images. Don't look, don't search, don't wrack your imagination for the right details.

Now, the little narration that you have patched together for this class exercise is most likely a horrible mess, but I hope you will get some laughs out of reading the results. Feel free to destroy your papers, if you think the ritual will mean something. Otherwise, keep it around to remind yourself of some of the things you don't want to do.

FIELD EXERCISE

This time when you observe people, observe them with the vices we have talked about in mind. Find somebody, or some scene, that would lend itself to writing full of a particular vice. For a very simple example, if you see somebody crying, you can imagine that scene being rendered in predictably sentimental romance prose.

You don't have to write the actual passages. Just record the scene and assign it a literary vice; then bring it back to the class. Class discussion can then center on how the opportunity to be bad might be avoided, and how the passage in question might actually be good.

SCRAPBOOK EXERCISE

Writers need to be aware of the quality of their thoughts. The scrapbook exercise for this chapter will help you watch out for thoughts that can make you a bad writer. In other words, you will find spaces to list shallow thoughts, dishonest thoughts, cruel thoughts, and sentimental thoughts that might go through your head. There's nothing wrong with having thoughts like those, as long as you learn to recognize them for what they are.

READING EXERCISE

Nobody's perfect. Here and there in your current reading, you are going to find something deplorable. Without being obsessive, keep your eye out for it. Even the greatest writers have faults, although those faults are balanced out by original virtues. Ask yourself what you see in your reading that can be called a vice. Be prepared to talk about whether your author compensates for that vice by means of some overriding virtue.

SUGGESTIONS FOR CURRENT PROJECT

I wish I could tell you that I had a formula that made it as easy to write well as it is to do these intentional bad-writing exercises. Unfortunately, it's not so. Good writing is by nature anti-formulaic, so there can never be formulae, only suggestions and words of encouragement.

The most encouraging thing I can tell you right now is that writing comes hard to everybody who is any good. In fact, I've heard a writer defined as someone for whom writing is harder than it is for most people.

If this course up to now has been more or less easy for you, then you're either not taking it at all seriously or you have absolutely no talent. If it's hard for you—if you're struggling and only hitting the mark once in a while—then you're about right.

Just keep up with your project. Work on it every day. Keep reading. Get as much feedback as you can from friends and classmates. Pay particular attention to the next chapter, which deals with the important topic of revision. That's as much of a formula as I can give you.

13

❖

Second, Third, Fourth, Fifth,
Sixth Chances, and So On:
The Joys and Sorrows of Revision

PURPOSE OF CHAPTER

In the early part of a class it's more important to get a sense of momentum going than to have people continually rehashing and resubmitting work that has been minimally revised. So the previous chapters haven't dealt much with revision, beyond reminding you to put some notes into your first drafts that you can come back to later.

Well, now it's later. And you should have established enough of your own momentum so that you can backtrack and rethink what you've been doing.

If you're lucky, your first drafts will have some life to them—but in general even the most accomplished writers will do well just to get a shadowy approximation of what they want on the first try.

That's why almost all writers have been fanatical revisers. You just don't get it right the first time. Or the second time. Writers often have big egos, but a real writer is never really satisfied.

The good part is that once you realize that there's nothing to be afraid of, revision is fun. For some writers it's much more fun than writing a first draft. It's very satisfying to see a passage go from being so-so to being truly alive. And it's nice to know that you can keep trying for as many drafts as you like. Baseball players only get three chances; you get as many as you want.

Now, I must tell you, there *is* one alternative to revision. That alternative is to have an I.Q. of at least 250. There were some (possibly unreliable) reports from Shakespeare's time that the Bard "never scratched a line."

For us mortals, though, revision is crucial.

Let's look first at the word itself. "Re-vision" actually means "re-seeing." It doesn't just mean tinkering, changing a word here and there.

The first thing I do to revise is make a printout from my computer, thus seeing the material from a different perspective than on the screen. Then I read it, and then I start asking questions.

1. Is it interesting?
2. Does it have a central problem?
3. Are the characters vividly drawn?
4. Are the characters illustrated by their own words and actions?
5. Is the setting someplace that the reader can imagine and visualize?
6. Are the details rendered specifically?
7. Is the dialogue readable and believable?
8. Does the story build on itself, with one plot development leading to another?
9. Is the language interesting without being show-offish?

Questions like these are the questions that lead to real revision, rather than computer tinkering. Don't be the kind of student who resubmits printouts identical to the first draft, except for one or two words that have to be pointed out to the instructor.

And here's a place where the labor-saving aspects of word processing can become a problem. Computers make it too easy to leave a dull or defective paragraph in your file and to keep printing it out again and again in the course of minuscule revisions.

When you are working with a computer, it is important to remember: *Don't let material stand by default.* If you feel stymied with a revision, print it out, then *delete the file.* Now start typing from scratch, with nothing to go by but your hard copy, making your own judgments as you go along. That way nothing gets in solely because it was in a previous draft. You'd be surprised what opportunities you discover when you're forced to get right back to the word-for-word original.

When computers began to play an important part in people's writing, many experts thought they would lead to the "paperless office." This hasn't happened, and maybe that's bad news for trees, but it's good news for you. Soothe your conscience by using paper made from recycled materials—but feel free to make as many printouts as you want; they help you see the material more clearly.

In this chapter we'll go through some exercises to help you learn to revise, and to help you establish good revision habits. Some of this can be done in class, or with your friends, but much of it remains a solitary process.

CLASS EXERCISE

Bring in enough of your current project to class so that whoever reads it will get some of a sense of what it's about. For a designated portion of the class time, students should give their projects to another student, who will read it and insert *at least ten questions* in the manuscript. Point out mechanical problems, but remember that this is not a matter of *editing* (I'll get to editing in the next chapter). This is a matter of *seeing* what the work is and what it can be. So make no comments other than to ask questions about the work you are looking at. You'll be doing your classmate a favor if you are forthright. Ask tough, searching questions.

Then take your own work home and look at it and see if you can answer the questions that have been given to you.

SCRAPBOOK EXERCISE

The exercise in the scrapbook supplement will ask you to list your classmate's questions, and to answer them as best you can. Then ask yourself what you most need, and see if you can answer that question.

SUGGESTIONS FOR CURRENT PROJECT

Every writer has to find a workable revision style. Some never go on to the next paragraph until the present one is perfect. Others dash through a whole book without looking back, then start revising from the beginning. Most find a technique somewhere in between those two extremes. Find your own way.

Remember, revision can be a joy, but it can also be very stressful. Sometimes you will have a passage in your work that you will be very fond of. It may be your favorite passage in the whole piece. Then, over the course of thinking and rethinking, you will begin to realize that, even though you like it, it needs to go away.

How you handle that moment says a lot about how you are shaping up as a writer. If you self-indulgently hang onto passages just because you are personally attached to them, you are being a wimp. But if you go ahead and lose something you like, even though it hurts (and it will hurt sometimes), then you might have some potential, in which case you should go on to the next chapter.

14

❖

Conclusion: Succeeding as a Writer

This workbook is primarily intended to help beginning writers get a handle on their craft. It's not a professional manual. But even beginning writers can benefit from asking themselves some hard questions about what they expect from the work they are doing.

How do you define success as a writer? By money? I hope you don't. The number of Americans who make enough money writing to support themselves is very small. By fame? Again, many wonderful writers never become a household word, except perhaps in their own households.

The only real yardstick for success that I know, the only principle not slavishly tied to the whims of the bestseller list and the currents of pop culture, must be internal. You need to ask yourself: what do *you* want out of it?

Some writers are happy to write for themselves alone, and never to let another soul see their work. Some content themselves by sharing their writing with friends and family, usually a "pre-sold" and very receptive audience.

But writing is communication, and the more people you communicate with the more effective you are. So it is natural to want to publish. And it's worth it, even if you don't get paid. To see your own work for the first time in real book or magazine type instead of the typescript in which you sent it is a thrill. It legitimizes you.

YOUR PUBLISHING PLAN

First of all, don't feel pressured. If you don't think you're ready to publish anything, or if you just don't care, you shouldn't feel obligated to go through the motions. You might want instead to save these instructions for a future time when you have something you think is closer to being saleable.

Even for those writers who do care about it, matters of publication should never occupy more than a fraction of their time.

Serious writers should own as many reference books as possible. So I'm not going to use this book to tell you things that other books tell much better. If you want to publish anything, you need to own at least a few of the books I'll be talking about.

Here, in greatly abbreviated form, is a list of the questions that might come up in the process of getting started publishing.

How Do I Know It's Ready?

On one level, you never do. That uncertainty goes with the territory. But by this time you should at least have something that you've taken as far as you can and that you think has some merit.

Then you need to have a well-edited manuscript. Remember that editing is not the same as revising. I'm talking about correctness now, about a scrupulously clean manuscript, free of spelling errors, punctuation errors, misprints, or other problems. You should already own a handbook to help you with editing questions. The *MLA Style Manual* and the *Chicago Manual of Style* are sources that the editors themselves refer to.

Where Should I Submit?

One of the happiest things about the writing business today is the number and variety of venues that exist for beginning writers. You can find numerous lists and description of those venues in several publications. The best known is the annual *Writer's Market*, along with the supplemental *Novel and Short Story Writer's Market*. These list hundreds of possible homes for your work, often along with an indication of how receptive the publication is to previously unpublished writers. Other annuals include *Writer's Yearbook* and *Literary Market Place*.

Yearly short story anthologies often include a list of the periodicals in which the included stories first appeared. Such lists can give you an early indication of which magazines are most respected in the publishing business.

What Should It Look Like?

The format should be standard: tricks or gimmicks or oversize titles mark you as an amateur, as a "little old lady from Dubuque." One particularly helpful publication is *The Writer's Digest Book of Manuscript Formats*, which provides detailed instructions on page setup, margins, headings, and pagination. Other books, such as *Writer's Market*, also provide some format guidelines.

The basic thing you want to remember is that visually, your manuscript should look exactly like every other manuscript your editor gets. All the originality should be in the writing.

What's the Etiquette?

All you need is your manuscript, a brief and polite cover letter *addressed to an individual editor, not "Dear Editor"*, and a self-addressed stamped return envelope big enough to comfortably return the manuscript. Your cover letter need not say much; it's just a polite social introduction. Don't brag, don't "kiss up," and above all don't explain what your work is about.

For short stories your envelope only needs to be a nine-by-twelve inch Manila envelope. For book-length manuscripts it's customary to use a box, like the box good typing paper comes in, and pack it in a padded "Jiffy bag."

Make use of your reference material. If you have any questions about submission etiquette, you should be able to find helpful answers there.

Then What?

Then you wait. Sometimes with quarterlies and "little magazines" you wait a long time. But there's a very effective antidote to the anxiety of waiting, and that's to produce more material. The feeling of always having a few pieces "out there," being read perhaps right now in somebody's office far away—that's a good feeling.

Eventually you'll hear from your editor. Sometimes you'll get a small letter. That's usually good news, meaning they're taking the manuscript.

More often than not, what you get back is your own SASE, containing your manuscript and a printed rejection slip. It always hurts a little to get those rejection slips, even when you know it's part of the business.

Some writers throw their rejection slips away. I think that's a bad idea. If you write seriously and you give it some effort, you're going to receive rejection slips. I think you should save them, paper your wall with them. After you've looked at them for a while they lose their negative force. Just remember that even the most successful writers get many rejection slips for every one acceptance.

A Submission Ledger

Some of your references might contain a sheet like this, but if they don't, here's one you can use to keep records of such things as submissions, editor's names and addresses, and the results of each submission. You should probably make a photocopy of it and stick it up near your desk.

Alternately, I wouldn't be surprised if some software company publishes a computer version of this ledger. That would keep your records a lot more neatly. Check around.

Submission Ledger

Name _____   *Date Begun* _____

Title of ms	Magazine	Editor	Address	Sent	Reply	Result

Appendix

❖

A Writer's Scrapbook

The scrapbook section of *The Hands-On Fiction Workbook* is included so that you can have a place to save some of the notes and memos you will be writing to yourself over the course of using the workbook. Every chapter but the last has a scrapbook exercise associated with it. Just turn to the Scrapbook Appendix when you are doing your chapter assignments and fill in the requested information.

Feel free to come back to these sections again and again. Use the space on the back of the pages for extra writing if you want. The best thing that could happen to you would be to develop the habit of keeping a scrapbook on your own after you are through working with this book.

NOTES

SCRAPBOOK EXERCISE FOR CHAPTER 1: GETTING STARTED

Here's the place to start thinking about what you'd like to achieve in this class. Just write something in response. Feel free to come back and change what you've written.

WHAT KIND OF A WRITER DO YOU WANT TO BE?

_____

_____

_____

WHAT KIND OF A WRITER DO YOU NOT WANT TO BE?

_____

_____

_____

WRITE DOWN AT LEAST FIVE THINGS YOU WANT YOUR WORK TO DO

1. _____

2. _____

3. _____

4. _____

5. _____

6. _____

7. _____

8. _____

9. _____

10. _____

NOTES

SCRAPBOOK EXERCISE FOR CHAPTER 2: KEEPING NOTES ON YOUR READING

Use this section of the appendix to keep a record of everything you read during the time you are using the workbook. Writing down responses to your reading, even very free-form responses, will help you remember what you read and may help your reading to influence your writing. Just write down the name of the book or story, and then write whatever you choose as a response.

Books

1. TITLE

   _____

   REMARKS/REACTIONS

   _____
   _____
   _____
   _____
   _____
   _____
   _____

2. TITLE

   _____

   REMARKS/REACTIONS

   _____
   _____
   _____
   _____
   _____
   _____
   _____

NOTES

3. TITLE

_____

REMARKS/REACTIONS

_____
_____
_____
_____
_____
_____
_____

4. TITLE

_____

REMARKS/REACTIONS

_____
_____
_____
_____
_____
_____

5. TITLE

_____

REMARKS/REACTIONS

_____
_____
_____
_____
_____
_____
_____

NOTES

_____

_____

_____

_____

_____

_____

_____

_____

_____

_____

_____

_____

_____

_____

_____

_____

_____

_____

_____

_____

_____

_____

_____

_____

_____

_____

_____

_____

Stories

1. TITLE

   _____

   REMARKS/REACTIONS

   _____
   _____
   _____
   _____
   _____
   _____

2. TITLE

   _____

   REMARKS/REACTIONS

   _____
   _____
   _____
   _____
   _____
   _____

3. TITLE

   _____

   REMARKS/REACTIONS

   _____
   _____
   _____
   _____
   _____
   _____

NOTES

_____

_____

_____

_____

_____

_____

_____

_____

_____

_____

_____

_____

_____

_____

_____

_____

_____

_____

_____

_____

_____

_____

_____

_____

_____

_____

_____

_____

4. TITLE

_____

REMARKS/REACTIONS

_____
_____
_____
_____
_____
_____

5. TITLE

_____

REMARKS/REACTIONS

_____
_____
_____
_____
_____
_____

6. TITLE

_____

REMARKS/REACTIONS

_____
_____
_____
_____
_____
_____

NOTES

7. TITLE

_____

REMARKS/REACTIONS

_____
_____
_____
_____
_____
_____

8. TITLE

_____

REMARKS/REACTIONS

_____
_____
_____
_____
_____
_____

9. TITLE

_____

REMARKS/REACTIONS

_____
_____
_____
_____
_____
_____

NOTES

10. TITLE

_____

REMARKS/REACTIONS

_____

_____

_____

_____

_____

_____

_____

NOTES

SCRAPBOOK EXERCISE FOR CHAPTER 3:
PROBLEMS THAT PROPEL STORIES

Think of the exercises in this section of the Scrapbook Appendix as an extension of the previous chapter. Keep thinking about the fiction you are reading in connection with the class, but here, instead of general comments, see if you can identify the central problem that drives the narrative. Even in the most seemingly shapeless avant-garde work you will always find a problem that moves the story. Just identify that problem as clearly as you can in everything you are reading.

Books

1. TITLE

   _____

   PROBLEM THAT DRIVES THE STORY

   _____
   _____
   _____
   _____
   _____
   _____
   _____

2. TITLE

   _____

   PROBLEM THAT DRIVES THE STORY

   _____
   _____
   _____
   _____
   _____
   _____
   _____

NOTES

3. TITLE

_____

PROBLEM THAT DRIVES THE STORY

_____
_____
_____
_____
_____
_____
_____

4. TITLE

_____

PROBLEM THAT DRIVES THE STORY

_____
_____
_____
_____
_____
_____

5. TITLE

_____

PROBLEM THAT DRIVES THE STORY

_____
_____
_____
_____
_____
_____

NOTES

Stories

1. TITLE

   _____

   PROBLEM THAT DRIVES THE STORY

   _____
   _____
   _____
   _____
   _____
   _____

2. TITLE

   _____

   PROBLEM THAT DRIVES THE STORY

   _____
   _____
   _____
   _____
   _____
   _____

3. TITLE

   _____

   PROBLEM THAT DRIVES THE STORY

   _____
   _____
   _____
   _____
   _____
   _____

NOTES

4. TITLE

_____

PROBLEM THAT DRIVES THE STORY

_____
_____
_____
_____
_____
_____

5. TITLE

_____

PROBLEM THAT DRIVES THE STORY

_____
_____
_____
_____
_____
_____

6. TITLE

_____

PROBLEM THAT DRIVES THE STORY

_____
_____
_____
_____
_____
_____

NOTES

7. TITLE

_____

PROBLEM THAT DRIVES THE STORY

_____
_____
_____
_____
_____
_____

8. TITLE

_____

PROBLEM THAT DRIVES THE STORY

_____
_____
_____
_____
_____
_____

9. TITLE

_____

PROBLEM THAT DRIVES THE STORY

_____
_____
_____
_____
_____
_____

NOTES

10. TITLE

_____

PROBLEM THAT DRIVES THE STORY

_____

_____

_____

_____

_____

_____

NOTES

SCRAPBOOK EXERCISE FOR CHAPTER 4:
ANECDOTE WORKSHEET

Use this space to make notes for a well-organized anecdote that you can share with the class. It can be a joke, a personal experience, or something you've heard from somebody else. Think about what you can do to hold your audience's interest.

ANECDOTE WORKSHEET

_____

_____

_____

_____

_____

_____

_____

_____

_____

_____

_____

_____

_____

_____

_____

_____

_____

_____

_____

_____

_____

_____

_____

_____

_____

NOTES

SCRAPBOOK EXERCISE FOR CHAPTER 5:
OBSERVING CHARACTERS

Use this space to describe the two strangers you have observed. Give them names of your own choosing, and speculate about what kind of characters they might make.

1. Character's name

   _____

   General description

   _____

   _____

   _____

   Most important physical characteristic

   _____

   _____

   _____

   Most important emotional characteristic

   _____

   _____

   _____

   How do you feel about this character?

   _____

   _____

   _____

   Is this a positive or a negative character?

   _____

   _____

   _____

NOTES

2. Character's name

_____

General description

_____

_____

_____

Most important physical characteristic

_____

_____

_____

Most important emotional characteristic

_____

_____

_____

How do you feel about this character?

_____

_____

_____

Is this a positive or a negative character?

_____

_____

_____

NOTES

SCRAPBOOK EXERCISE FOR CHAPTER 6:
THINGS THAT REVEAL CHARACTER

List three people you know well, and see if you can identify the crucial expression, gesture or mannerism that reveals each one's character.

1. Person's name

   _____

   Thing that reveals character

   _____
   _____
   _____   _____
   _____
   _____

2. Person's name

   _____

   Thing that reveals character

   _____
   _____
   _____
   _____
   _____

3. Person's name

   _____

   Thing that reveals character

   _____
   _____
   _____
   _____
   _____

NOTES

SCRAPBOOK EXERCISE FOR CHAPTER 7: FOUND DIALOGUE

Keep listening to conversations, and use the space below to record interesting, strange, funny, or particularly meaningful dialogue exchanges that you have heard. Use extra pages if necessary.

_____

_____

_____

_____

_____

_____

_____

_____

_____

_____

_____

_____

_____

_____

_____

_____

_____

_____

_____

_____

_____

_____

_____

_____

_____

_____

_____

NOTES

NOTES

SCRAPBOOK EXERCISE FOR CHAPTER 8: UNDERSTANDING PLOT BY WRITING *TV GUIDE*-STYLE BLURBS

Choose your three favorite books and write a fifteen or twenty word description of them, in the style of *TV Guide*. You should be able to catch the gist and the spirit of the story in that brief description.

   1. Title

      _____

      Blurb

      _____

      _____

      _____

      _____

      _____

      _____

      (Number of words in blurb_____)

   2. Title

      _____

      Blurb

      _____

      _____

      _____

      _____

      _____

      _____

      _____

      (Number of words in blurb_____)

NOTES

3. Title

_____

Blurb

_____

_____

_____

_____

_____

_____

_____

(Number of words in blurb_____)

NOTES

SCRAPBOOK EXERCISE FOR CHAPTER 9: THINGS YOU'VE NEVER NOTICED BEFORE

This exercise asks you to stretch your powers of perception and to observe familiar things from a writer's perspective, looking for things about them that you've never noticed before. If you're trying to find out something new about a person you know or a place nearby, you might want to visit that person or place, so as to jog your imagination.

Here's the list.

Name of person

_____

What I never noticed before

_____

_____

_____

_____

My home (description)

_____

What I never noticed before

_____

_____

_____

_____

Somebody's car

_____

What I never noticed before

_____

_____

_____

_____

NOTES

School or workplace

_____

What I never noticed before

_____

_____

_____

_____

This town

_____

What I never noticed before

_____

_____

_____

_____

My favorite song

_____

What I never noticed before

_____

_____

_____

_____

A celebrity

_____

What I never noticed before

_____

_____

_____

_____

NOTES

SCRAPBOOK EXERCISE FOR CHAPTER 10: MAKING PLACES REAL

Make a list of at least five places that you have feelings about, either positive or negative. See if you can say what single thing makes them what they are.

1. Place

   _____

   _____

   _____

   What makes it special?

   _____

   _____

   _____

   What have you noticed about it that nobody else has?

   _____

   _____

   _____

   How do you feel about the place?

   _____

   _____

   _____

   How could it be altered so as to become a promising fictional setting?

   _____

   _____

   _____

   What kind of story could most naturally take place here?

   _____

   _____

   _____

NOTES

2. Place

_____

_____

_____

What makes it special?

_____

_____

_____

_____

What have you noticed about it that nobody else has?

_____

_____

_____

_____

How do you feel about the place?

_____

_____

_____

_____

How could it be altered so as to become a promising fictional setting?

_____

_____

_____

_____

What kind of story could most naturally take place here?

_____

_____

_____

_____

NOTES

3. Place

_____

_____

_____

What makes it special?

_____

_____

_____

_____

What have you noticed about it that nobody else has?

_____

_____

_____

_____

How do you feel about the place?

_____

_____

_____

_____

How could it be altered so as to become a promising fictional setting?

_____

_____

_____

_____

What kind of story could most naturally take place here?

_____

_____

_____

_____

NOTES

4. Place

_____

_____

_____

What makes it special?

_____

_____

_____

_____

What have you noticed about it that nobody else has?

_____

_____

_____

_____

How do you feel about the place?

_____

_____

_____

_____

How could it be altered so as to become a promising fictional setting?

_____

_____

_____

_____

What kind of story could most naturally take place here?

_____

_____

_____

_____

NOTES

5. Place

_____

_____

_____

What makes it special?

_____

_____

_____

_____

What have you noticed about it that nobody else has?

_____

_____

_____

_____

How do you feel about the place?

_____

_____

_____

_____

How could it be altered so as to become a promising fictional setting?

_____

_____

_____

_____

What kind of story could most naturally take place here?

_____

_____

_____

_____

NOTES

SCRAPBOOK EXERCISE FOR CHAPTER 11:
EXPLORING YOUR POINT-OF-VIEW PREFERENCES

Every writer has a favorite point of view. Take some time here to think about what yours is, about how well it has worked for you, and whether you need to do more experimentation.

1. What point of view are you most comfortable writing in?

   _____

   _____

2. In what story or passage has that point of view worked best for you?

   _____

   _____

3. What book or story using your preferred point of view do you admire most?

   _____

   _____

4. What point of view do you feel least comfortable with?

   _____

   _____

   _____

5. What do you think you would have to do to make that point of view work for you?

   _____

   _____

   _____

6. In what kind of book or story do you think this other point of view could work well?

   _____

   _____

   _____

NOTES

SCRAPBOOK EXERCISE FOR CHAPTER 12: WATCHING OUT FOR THOUGHTS THAT CAN MAKE YOU A BAD WRITER

Here's a list of the kinds of thoughts that can cheapen your vision and diminish your ability to perceive the world in an generous manner. Try to be aware when you have such a thought, and summarize it here, so that you'll know it for what it is.

1. Shallow and easy thoughts

   _____

   _____

   _____ _____

   _____

   _____

   _____

   _____

   _____

   _____

   _____

   _____

2. Dishonest thoughts

   _____

   _____

   _____

   _____

   _____

   _____

   _____

   _____

   _____

   _____

NOTES

3. Frigid or cruel thoughts

_____

_____

_____

_____

_____

_____

_____

_____

4. Sentimental thoughts

_____

_____

_____

_____

_____

_____

_____

_____

5. Self-indulgent thoughts

_____

_____

_____

_____

_____

_____

_____

_____

NOTES

SCRAPBOOK EXERCISE FOR CHAPTER 13: QUESTIONS TO HELP YOU REVISE YOUR WORK

Use the space here to list the most important questions that your fellow students have raised. Then see if you can answer the questions.

1. Question

   _____

   _____

   _____

   Possible answer

   _____

   _____

   _____

2. Question

   _____

   _____

   _____

   Possible answer

   _____

   _____

   _____

3. Question

   _____

   _____

   _____

   Possible answer

   _____

   _____

   _____

NOTES

4. Question

_____

_____

_____

Possible answer

_____

_____

_____

5. Question

_____

_____

_____

Possible answer

_____

_____

_____

6. Question

_____

_____

_____

Possible answer

_____

_____

_____

NOTES

7. Question

Possible answer

8. Question

Possible answer

9. Question

Possible answer

NOTES

10. Question

_____

_____

_____

Possible answer

_____

_____

_____

NOTES

Index